PERSIUS: THE SATIRES

PERSIUS Flaccus, Aulus

(The Satires)

Text with Translation and Notes by

J. R. Jenkinson

British Library Cataloguing in Publication Data

Persius Flaccus, Aules
  [Satires. English and Latin] . Persius.
  I. Title   II. Jenkinson, J R
  871'.01   PA6555.A2

  ISBN 0-85668-159-8 *cloth*
      0-85668-173-3 *paperback*

Published by ARIS & PHILLIPS LTD, Warminster, Wiltshire, England.

Printed in England by BIDDLES LTD, Guildford, Surrey.

CONTENTS

PREFACE

Persius is a stimulating but difficult poet. I hope that students who work with no knowledge, or no very ready knowledge, of the Latin tongue and other students too may find this book an interesting and useful source of information about the poet's work and about the varied interpretations of detail which it has called forth from editors. I hope, too, that the general reader, ignoring as much as he wishes of the Notes and the Appendixes, may gain acquaintance with an unusual classical writer.

Because other and very lucid English versions are available, I felt encouraged, in writing the Translation, to try for what I take to be the unapologetic and adventurous brevity and inexplicitness of Persius' expression. The extensive annotation is, in its major part, a result of his frequent reference to matters of life, language and literature which were familiar to contemporaries and go unexplained in the text, but are unfamiliar to us. Often it seemed best to write a single long note on the topic or group of topics to which a number of points in a passage were related, and at each point to guide the reader, by a repeated reference number, to the one note. Since the Translation often involved, as is alike inevitable and desirable, the preference of one possible version and the rejection of others, some sections of the Notes and the majority of the Appendixes deal with matters of interpretation that are subject to discussion or controversy. While notes and appendixes may help towards a fuller grasp of Persius' precise meaning, and while the Translation without them would be incomplete, the best initial assessment of the poems' impact may well proceed from a reading which pauses as little as possible to attend to their explanations. The reader is encouraged at least to try such an approach as he or she might use towards modern unannotated poetry whose meaning is not immediately clear.

I wish to thank very much all who at various points have helped, advised or encouraged me, especially Dr A. W. Bower, Dr C. W. Chilton, Mr. L. E. Donnelly, Professors D. C. Earl and G. P. Goold, Mr. J. Hilton, Dr. S. Ireland, Professors A. F. Norman and A. Pollard, Dr. T. T. B. Ryder, Mr. J. C. G. Strachan, Professors E. H. Warmington and A. Watson, and the advisers of Aris & Phillips Ltd. I have had great help, too, from the officers of the Brynmor Jones Library, especially Mrs. K. A. Holbrook, Mr. D. J. Orton and Mr. P. Sheldon; from those of other libraries who communicated information by post (see CQ 29.1979.146, n.); and from the editors of TLL. Permission to use Professor W. V. Clausen's 1956 text of Persius has kindly been accorded by the Oxford University Press, and I would express my gratitude both to them and to him. Miss H. Thompson, Mrs. G. Smith, Mrs. D. Williams and her staff and Mrs. P. Moore have all given generous and patient help with typing. Finally, I wish to thank my wife Beatrice and daughters Katie, Rachel and Helen, whose help and whose gentle patience and resignation contributed to every word of the book. To them and *magistris mortuis* Leslie Burgess and A. N. Bryan-Brown it is offered.

J. R. Jenkinson
Hull, October 1979

INTRODUCTION

The full name of the author whose work is translated below was Aules[1]
Persius Flaccus. He has left us (not counting a brief introductory piece) six Latin
poems of moderate length in the hexameter metre. Their title, *Saturae,* is usually
translated 'Satires' which, as we shall see, is technically correct. But, influenced
as we are by modern presuppositions about the word 'satire', we might feel that
'Sermons' or 'Moral Essays' were titles more aptly descriptive of their main content.

Persius belonged to the well-to-do and landowning gentry of Italy.[2] He
lived between 34 and 62 A.D., passing his adult life under the emperors Claudius
and Nero. He was educated in Rome at the best schools; then, as Romans some-
times did in the course of their education,[3] he undertook the study of philosophy,
attaching himself as pupil to Annaeus Cornutus, an eminent Stoic philosopher,
teacher and writer.[4] The tone and philosophical content of the Satires suggest
that he pursued philosophy with an ardour beyond that conventionally thought
proper by Romans.[5]

Some details in the ancient *Life* (see n. 2) suggest that previously he had
had aspirations, and had been subject to family influences, which turned him in
the direction of philosophy. He was related to the two ladies Arria, the elder of
whom was famous for her heroic suicide. This occurred when Persius was eight
or thereabouts, and he wrote a boyhood poem in her honour. The younger, her
daughter, was wife to the Stoic senator and martyr Thrasea Paetus. Through her,
it seems, he had the *entrée* to Thrasea's house, company and friendship.

Stoicism was a respected philosophy and probably enjoyed a wider follow-
ing than any western pre-Christian school of thought. It was an elaborate philo-
sophical system whose adherents, especially in the age when Persius lived,
advocated and followed its ethical doctrines with a zeal that was virtually religious.
The Stoics taught that the universe is divine, intelligible and benevolent and that
the individual, by training, care and thought, may know what its nature is and
how properly to relate himself and his actions to it. In particular he may under-
stand what is good, and that virtuous states and actions are the supreme good for
him. Virtue consists in the proper adjustment of the will to the benevolent Law
or Will that informs the universe; and, since virtue resides in the realm of the will
and is the true good, it follows that everything which can truly benefit or harm

1

a man is under his own control. Anything external to the control of his will, including considerations such as health, freedom, fame, prosperity and their opposites, the seeking or avoidance of which cause all human passions and sorrows, is not a fit thing for the Stoic to take account of, to be attracted or repelled by. He is, in fact, morally and emotionally independent: '. . . a whole in himself, smooth and rounded, so that nothing external can rest on his polished surface, against whom Fortune, in her onset, is ever maimed.' '. . . Were the vault of heaven to break and fall upon him, it would strike him undismayed.' [6] In view of the extent, still more restricted then than now, of man's control of his destiny, the attraction of a philosophy giving this spiritual foothold and orientation is easy to understand. The ramifying details of its ethical teaching and the spirit in which this was carried out can best be experienced by reading Stoic works which are roughly contemporary with Persius, for example the letters of Seneca or the sermons of Epictetus and Musonius Rufus.[7] They will be found to bear at least a family likeness to the topics and tone of Persius' philosophical poetry.

Stoicism had grown up in the Hellenistic world and was perhaps shaped according to the spiritual needs of the ordinary citizen, who was uninvolved and unimportant in the taking of decisions that affected and controlled his community. It is perhaps natural that it should also include among its many adherents a section of the upper echelons of Roman society during the reigns of Nero and his immediate predecessors and successors. The upper class not only felt itself starved of real political influence but in addition was humiliatingly compelled to hold debate in the senate as if it possessed powers of important decision, and was subjected to the fear that its actions, especially any endeavour to assert real independence, would incur the Emperor's suspicion. Honest men may well have been concerned with a search for self-respect and spiritual direction.

It seems likely that from the beginning of his reign Nero's conduct was not such as to inspire confidence in those whose nominal share in government might call upon them to condone his acts. Persius' friend Thrasea, whose parents-in-law had already suffered death in a conflict with the Throne, chose to hold aloof from elements in the senate which gave eager and exaggerated demonstrations of loyalty, and in 59 A.D. risked the emperor's severe displeasure by a public act of implicit criticism.[8] A degree of foreboding and isolation, which had its fulfilment only later,[9] seems likely to have affected the quality of life for Thrasea, his associates and dependants already in Persius' lifetime.

Of all this Persius' poems convey nothing, unless, as seems possible, the political and social environment was in part responsible for their taut sense of the importance of Stoic moral principles. Of the six major poems in his collection, the first deals with Roman tastes and *mores* in literary matters, and the rest with selected tenets of conventional Stoic doctrine which Persius will have met in private study or in technical or hortatory lectures. And, although it would have been possible to give themes such as the honour of the gods (poem 2), political precocity (poem 4) and moral freedom (poem 5) a topical application, this is missing. His moralising seeks a high level of abstraction from historical events. It is important to realise that his failure to engage in topical comment and polemic is not quite the departure from the traditions of his chosen genre that the modern sense of the title 'Satire(s)' would suggest.

The Latin term *satura* [10] was probably in origin a title, meaning 'Miscellany', aptly used by the genre's earliest practitioners to denote a collection of poems that recorded details of the poet's personal experiences and opinions in a wide variety of fields. The poems were written in a lively manner and were illustrated with descriptive and dramatic episodes. Not unnaturally the collections included, among numberless other topics, the consideration of moral themes in the manner of the prevailing philosophies. [11]

Lucilius (? 168/7 - 103/2 B.C.), the first major, and in fact the most miscellaneous, writer of *satura*, had a personality which, given freedom by his high social status and connections, brought into his poetry an element of pungent topical criticism of morals and politics of a type not uncommon in republican Roman literature. It was perhaps owing to the influence of his work and a certain notoriety which these elements in it enjoyed, that *satura* as a genre-name became associated especially with morals and with topical polemic. [12]

However, the tone of comment and the type of *satura* which authors aspired to write varied much, and it seems likely that among factors which influenced them was their estimate of what it was possible to write in the social and political environment in which they worked, and what was proper to their social station.

Horace (65-8 B.C.) was the son of a freedman and, when he wrote, the dependant of Augustus. His *satura* offers little if anything that could be described as political comment, is usually restrained in moral criticism and lays emphasis rather upon general moral theses than upon the castigation of particular present situations or of individuals. The names of persons, where he uses them in criticism, are not those of powerful men and are often fictitious. Also he varied the content of his collection with poems of autobiography, anecdote and literary criticism, probably in an endeavour to broaden the concept of the genre and diminish its association with hostile moral criticism by calling back to life and memory the idea of 'miscellany' which had underlain Lucilius' work.

The Stoic preacher Crispinus who figures in Horace's satire also has interest. It seems legitimate to deduce from Horace's references to him [13] that whatever the public might expect, writings which tended to a general, non-hostile, consideration of ethics could properly be classed as *satura.*

The title of Persius' work, then, did not promise any certain subject-matter or treatment to a Roman audience, apart from some concern with morals. The tone and method of moral discussion in *satura* had, in practice, varied considerably, and his sermons bore a family likeness to the practice of other authors in the genre. His literary poem also has a function that was traditional in *satura* (see Sat. 1, n. 1).

It is clear that the pressures of life under an autocracy made dangerous or unthinkable the wide dissemination, under an author's name, of the political polemic and of much of the pointed social satire that is possible in freer societies. [14] This would account for Persius' choice of an untopical kind of moral comment. On the other hand Persius was reasonably well-connected and he did, in his first poem, venture a portrait of Roman literary tastes, and incidentally of Roman morals, that (in our sense) satirises sections of contemporary society and certainly risked giving offence. Had he wished, it would have been possible for him, while running no significantly greater risk, to write topical moral counterparts to poem 1.[15] If in addition we remember details in the ancient *Life* which attest his devotion to those who taught him philosophy, [16] his own words on the subject early in poem 5 and the fervent tone of the moral poems as a whole, it is justifiable to believe that the presentation of Stoic doctrines as such, and in a universal way, was Persius' central desire, and that *satura* suggested itself as a natural and convenient form for his purpose. Since the *Life* tells us that he wrote ' . . . infrequently and slowly', it seems to be a desire that he pursued with virtually no change for a long period. A corollary of this is that he was never interested, at least to a comparable degree, in the actual public events and situations that are the stuff of topical comment. It seems unlikely that he can have been totally unaware of them. [17] He may have felt repelled or daunted by these aspects of life themselves, [18] rather than by the consequences of commenting upon them. In the event, however, the choice of Stoic themes in a small way representative of the doctrines that stiffened the opposition of the Roman Stoics in Nero's day makes the *Satires* as fair a memorial to them as some more topically-oriented work would have been.

We need now to ask, in what way has Persius written about his themes, and does the way in which he has written deserve favourable or adverse judgement? These are the crucial questions concerning Persius's *Satires.* His way of writing is, so far as we know, unique in ancient poetry. His basic themes and many at least of their details are drawn from established doctrine.[19] It is, then, only his mode of presentation which may be used to estimate his stature as a poet.

On the whole Persius has been coolly received in recent times, particularly on account of his lack of lucidity and the untopical nature of his moral writings.

However, he not only had warm admirers in antiquity, but was read with appreciation by English satirists at the end of the sixteenth century, who show his influence. [20] Further, the present century has seen poets gain repute whose meaning is no more immediately plain than Persius's. These facts suggest that discussions with a view to forming a fresh and detailed estimate of Persius' poetry are desirable. Most recently J. P. Sullivan has indicated lines along which criticism of his use of words can proceed and H. Bardon has written illuminatingly about his use of images. [21]

Images play a very important part in Persius' writing. They are ubiquitous and may be very vivid. Not infrequently there are moderately extended pieces of lucid descriptive or dramatic writing. On the other hand, an explicit framework of logical abstract argument may be totally lacking or may lack emphasis by comparison with the images. The effect of this is that the images are left to do duty in place of the expression of abstract thoughts: " . . . they do not clothe a thought . . . on the contrary the thoughts result . . . from the images." [22] At times they are of some length and complexity. Nevertheless, because they are single images, densely expressed and conveying relevant ideas, the effect is one of economy. Also the image chosen is often arrestingly curious and often apt. From these features of their imagery the poems derive great impact.

Further, the elements of composition in Persius' satires— words and ideas, images, steps in the argument, registers of speech and literary style, speeches in dramatic dialogue—are abruptly or peculiarly, even bizarrely, combined. One is faced by an unpredictable, surprising series of conceptions; continuous attention is necessary if one is to understand. However, the surprises and incongruities are often observably intelligent, apt and curiously artistic. [23]

From a literary point of view, the quality of continual surprise in Persius' style makes the *Satires* amusing to read, just as pieces of intellectual play by John Donne or Gerard Manley Hopkins are elements of one's pleasure in reading their poetry. Persius explored the possibilities of language and poetic expression, and what he achieved could have been a source of literary renewal. It is a pity that his bold experiments seem to have had little if any influence on the subsequent history of Latin poetry.

However, it is important to our evaluation of the poems that they should not be thought of predominantly as examples of literary ingenuity. Couched in an adventurous idiom and manifestly controlled by an intellectual and aesthetic purpose, the statements of Stoic doctrine, fervent and definite, but bare of detailed or deeply-reasoned support, become part of worthwhile artistic objects which have their own authority. Without this blending they would merely be effusions. Moreover, Persius' series of surprising juxtapositions means that the reader must either sacrifice his own, and all ordinary and prosaic modes of thought, or else give up his attempt to read, at least to read seriously.[24] The sacrifice, if made, allows him to give imaginative consideration to other modes of thought and to appreciate the poet's conceptions. These, by their combined peculiarity and vividness, are especially fitted to appeal to private quirks of a reader's mind and imagination; and, previously unimagined but now discovered, to convert themselves into his personal possession. In Persius, as in the writings of the two English poets mentioned above, elements which display intellectual and aesthetic control help to convey moral or religious content.

The moral concern which Persius shows in his Satires is for the conduct of life by the individual. His imagery, including the imagery in the narrative and descriptive examples that illustrate his work, is vivid and uses realistic detail, well-observed from life. But quite commonly the examples are not, as those of Horace and Juvenal commonly are, reports of *particular events,* viewed as happening or having happened, in which people's folly or wickedness is exemplified and made the target of social or topical criticism. Persius tends to use examples which are of a frankly general or imaginary nature, including literary and quasi-literary examples. Some of his images, including possibly his most vivid, are used not primarily as examples of misguided action, but as aids to better definition of philosophic principles (cf. 5.73-131) or to describe the sureness with which they operate (3.88-106). The characters in the examples are often involved in quite humble and ordinary situations. Dislike or condemnation may be apparent in the reporting, and there may be mild caricature, but usually the situations and events are not greatly exaggerated or sensationalised. Upon occasion specific and unexpectedly violent condemnation of these characters (e.g. at 2.39f., 3.15) makes clear the strength of Stoic principle and how universally its demands operate (cf. 5.119f.).[25] It is also made clear that ultimately it is not external show, even as constituted by the legalistic performance of duties, that is put to the test by these demands, but the posture of the mind (2.73f., 3.30, 5.93-9, 119-21, 157-60). And it is often implicit, and sometimes explicit, that a person's response to them is a critical matter, productive of beatitude or misery. There is, finally, a common and most significant tendency to phrase example-material in a way which permits or encourages the reader to imagine himself in the situation depicted. This is done predominantly by the use of second-person address, e.g. "You beg strength of muscle . . . " 2.41. "It's morning and you're snoring peacefully . . . " 5.132f.

To sum up: Satires 2-6 are forceful meditative sermons in which, together with the nature and importance of moral principles, situations for their application are imaginatively realised, and encouragement is offered to the reader to match

6

his own responses with those situations. The questions and areas of behaviour which the examples illuminate are relevant to the human predicament and individual action:- proper conduct towards the powers thought to control the Universe, attitudes to one's own powers, independence in the face of temptation, the use of one's personal resources, and (in Sat. 3) the importance of giving due and detailed consideration to all these things.

Finally we may discuss the extent to which the style of the *Satires* was influenced by their literary environment.

Persius' love of the unexpected has parallels in the Greco-Roman sermon tradition. [26] It would equally have been encouraged by the self-conscious stylists of rhetorical declamation, which was fashionable as public entertainment and also formed an essential part of education in Persius' day. [27] Persius' individuality is marked, however, by the frequency of unexpected elements in his writing, by the extreme forms of unexpectedness which he employed and, as we have seen, by the vital relationship of these qualities to the meaning and authority of the poems. Worthy of remark, too, is the absence of that luxuriant use of stylistic ornament which is characteristic of the declaimers, and of his contemporary Seneca. [28] It is consistent with the poems' sense of urgency and economy that this ornament should be lacking: for it commonly contributes to length without being strictly necessary to the content, and emphasises form rather than meaning. Persius' reaction to this tendency can be read at Sat.1.85-91.

In Satire I Persius gives us a view of his relationship to some contemporary types of poetry. Because of difficulties of interpretation his meaning at some points is not clear, but its general drift can hardly be in doubt; that subject-matter which has no connection with real life does not please his taste, and that to give it subtly artistic expression, no matter how attractive, is to aggravate a fault, not to cure it. The combination is degenerate and worthy of disgust. His own concern is with living and experience. Subtly smooth styles such as he rejects would be unnecessary and inappropriately matched to this content, and his own writing does not employ them. [29] He looks for inspiration to predecessors who were members of, or were associated with, the tradition of satiric criticism (Sat. 1. 114-25, Horace Sat.1.4.1ff.), and whose style and manners had different, rougher qualities.

Satire 5. 1-29 views with more than a hint of mockery and distrust the subjects and the exalted style of epic and tragic poetry. Thus Persius, while insisting that the genre *satura* and the matter and style associated with it are worthy of his choice, rejects a good proportion of contemporary poetry. On the other hand we have seen that his way of writing a traditionally personal, critical and colloquial [30] genre is very much his own; and in the early verses of Satire 5 he advances the claim

7

that a straightforward use of an exalted style of the type associated with tragedy and epic is appropriate when serious and worthwhile things are the subject of composition, such as his debt to the guidance of Cornutus. [31]

A note must be added concerning the relationship of Persius' satires to the writing of his famous predecessor in the *satura*-tradition, Horace.

In Latin verse allusion to eminent predecessors is a very common practice. Even so Persius still stands out for the frequency with which he alludes to Horace's works, the lyric as well as the satiric poems. The examples quoted in footnotes to the translation are only a tiny proportion of the cases which exist. [32] One necessary condition for the perfect English translation is that it should contain a similar number of allusions to the work of an English poet. A curious feature of the relationship, however, is that the light, tactful, ironic and sceptical Horatian manner, so well described by Persius at Sat. 1.116-18, is something like the opposite of the fervent and committed Stoic preaching of Persius in which all the allusions to Horace lie embedded. There would appear to be room for discussion of the nature, purposes and effects of this further example of juxtaposition in Persius.

Note:

Line-numbers in the margin of the Translation give an approximate reference to the lines of the **LATIN** text.

A. PERSI FLACCI SATURAE

THE SATIRES OF A. PERSIUS FLACCUS

PROLOGUS

nec fonte labra prolui caballino
nec in bicipiti somniasse Parnaso
memini, ut repente sic poeta prodirem.
Heliconidasque pallidamque Pirenen
illis remitto quorum imagines lambunt
hederae sequaces; ipse semipaganus
ad sacra vatum carmen adfero nostrum.
quis expedivit psittaco suum 'chaere'
picamque docuit nostra verba conari?
magister artis ingenique largitor
venter, negatas artifex sequi voces.
quod si dolosi spes refulserit nummi,
corvos poetas et poetridas picas
cantare credas Pegaseium nectar.

5

10

5   *relinquo* Φ
      ambiunt a, supra scr. P²
      post 8 subditivum versum, *corvos quis olim concavum salutare* exhibent
      qr Vat. Pal. 1710 (ff. 16ᵛ ss.), post 9 Lu
9   *picasque* ΦP² *conari*] 'et *blandiri* legitur' Σ
12   *refulgeat aCR*, 'et *refulgeat* (legitur)' Σ

PROLOGUE[1]

I never swilled my lips in Dobbin Spring[2] nor dreamed,
that I recall, upon Parnassus' twin peaks,[2] thence to step
forth suddenly a Poet. Helicon-maids and pale Pirene[3] I
leave to those whose busts the clinging ivies lick;[3] whilst   5
offering my poems at the Rituals of Minstrelsy,[4] a half-
member of its Chapel.[4]
    Who got the parrot his 'Hello there!'[5] and taught the
magpie to attempt our speech? — Doctor of Arts and Bestow-   10
er of genius, the Belly, that gifted searcher-out of words with-
held. And if there's the glittering prospect of perfidious cash,
you'd think the raven-poet and the magpie-poetess sang
Pegasian nectar.[6]

SATURA I

" 'o curas hominum! o quantum est in rebus inane!'
quis leget haec?" min tu istud ais? nemo hercule. "nemo?"
vel duo vel nemo. "turpe et miserabile." quare?
ne mihi Polydamas et Troiades Labeonem
5   praetulerint? nugae. non, si quid turbida Roma
elevet, accedas examenve inprobum in illa
castiges trutina nec te quaesiveris extra.
nam Romae quis non –? a, si fas dicere . . . sed fas
tunc cum ad canitiem et nostrum istud vivere triste
10   aspexi ac nucibus facimus quaecumque relictis,
cum sapimus patruos. tunc tunc—ignoscite . . . nolo,
quid faciam? . . . sed sum petulanti splene – cachinno.
   scribimus inclusi, numeros ille, hic pede liber,
grande aliquid quod pulmo animae praelargus anhelet.
15   scilicet haec populo pexusque togaque recenti
et natalicia tandem cum sardonyche albus
sede leges celsa, liquido cum plasmate guttur
mobile conlueris, patranti fractus ocello.
tunc neque more probo videas nec voce serena
20   ingentis trepidare Titos, cum carmina lumbum
intrant et tremulo scalpuntur ubi intima versu.
tun, vetule, auriculis alienis colligis escas,

1	*o* alterum om. Neps et ut vid. Σ
6	*-ve*] *-que* aMRW
8	*Romae est* PΦΣ *ac* PaΦ
14	*quo* aMx
16	*alvus* P Sang.
17	*legens* PaΦ
18	*colluerit* CNR
19	*hic* aΦΣ
22	*tunc* a et ante ras. x *aescam* Prisc. GLK II p. 107 (cod. Sang. 904)

SATIRE I

ON SATIRE, LITERATURE AND MORALS[1]

" 'Alas the woes of men, the vast, universal void!'[2] –
Who'll read that?"
    Is it me you're talking to? No one whatever.
"No one?"
Two at most.
"A pitiful disgrace!"
    Why? For fear Polydamas and Troy's Ladies[3] read Labeo[3]
instead of me? Piffle! If our disordered City thinks lightly of   5
anything, don't go to her side or adjust the faulty pointer [4]
on *those* scales. Don't look outside yourself: at Rome who's
not – oh if I might say it! – but I might, when I look at our
greybeard-severity of living and at all we do once we're out of   10
short pants[5] and savouring sagely of the Heavy Father:[5] oh
then – despite myself I can't resist; forgive me, but my ribs are
fiends for tickling – I laugh!
    We lock ourselves away and write – one in verse, foot-
free another – a sublime Something for lungs breeze-bounti-
ful to puff. And this you'll read to the public,[6] combed,   15
fresh-toga'd, wearing, now, your sardonyx-birthstone,[6]
white and set aloft. You'll have washed your agile throat
out with a clear *vibrato,* eyes coming-off, effeminate. Then
might you see sturdy citizens[7] quiver in unseemly style and   20
with unsteady voice as the poetry enters their loins and as
their inmost parts are fretted by the trembling verse. Collat-
ing dishes for others' ears that you, corrupt in ears and hide,

auriculis quibus et dicas cute perditus 'ohe'?
"quo didicisse, nisi hoc fermentum et quae semel intus
25   innata est rupto iecore exierit caprificus?"
en pallor seniumque! o mores, usque adeone
scire tuum nihil est nisi te scire hoc sciat alter?
"at pulchrum est digito monstrari et dicier 'hic est.'
ten cirratorum centum dictata fuisse
30   pro nihilo pendes?" ecce inter pocula quaerunt
Romulidae saturi quid dia poemata narrent.
hic aliquis, cui circum umeros hyacinthina laena est,
rancidulum quiddam balba de nare locutus,
Phyllidas, Hypsipylas, vatum et plorabile siquid
35   eliquat ac tenero subplantat verba palato.
adsensere viri: nunc non cinis ille poetae
felix? non levior cippus nunc inprimit ossa?
laudant convivae: nunc non e manibus illis,
nunc non e tumulo fortunataque favilla
40   nascentur violae? "rides," ait, "et nimis uncis
naribus indulges. an erit qui velle recuset
os populi meruisse et cedro digna locutus
linquere nec scombros metuentia carmina nec tus?"
quisquis es, o modo quem ex adverso dicere feci,
45   non ego cum scribo, si forte quid aptius exit —
quando haec rara avis est — si quid tamen aptius exit,
laudari metuam; neque enim mihi cornea fibra est;
sed recti finemque extremumque esse recuso
'euge' tuum et 'belle'. nam 'belle' hoc excute totum:
50   quid non intus habet? non hic est Ilias Atti
ebria veratro? non siqua elegidia crudi
dictarunt proceres? non quidquid denique lectis

---

23   *articulis* Madvig, Adversaria Critica II, p. 128, in utroque loco exhibet Vat. 3292
30   *pendas* aΦ
31   *quis . . . narret* a (*quis* x)
34   *vanum* P
36   *nunc nunc* eu et ut vid. M
37   *imprimat* GWs
40   *nascuntur* Lku
44   *fas est* aMR

would find too much!– old man, how could you?[8]

"Wherefore were all the lessons if this ferment, this
that has sprung up within, does not burst the guts and grow,   25
this wild fig-tree?"[9]

What price the scholar and sage? [10] Disgraceful! Does
knowing have so little worth unless you're known to know
such things?

"But it's glorious to be pointed to and have it said:
'That's him!' Can you think it worthless to have been the
set book in hundreds of satchels?" [11]

Behold, as the port circulates, Rome's glutted sons   30
enquire:

What has fair Poetry to say? [12]

Then someone in a lavender tuxedo [12] speaks a putrid
line or two from an inarticulate nose, lets filter forth
Phyllises, Hypsipyles, [13] whatever's full of woe and min-
streldom, and lays out the words along his dainty palate.   35

Approved by the gallant company! How blest are
those poet's embers now! How lessened the tombstone's
weight upon his bones! Applauded by poor relations! [14]
Now from those remains, that tomb, those ashes in bliss,
how violets shall spring! [15]   40

"Oh, you laugh!" comes the reply, "and let your lip
curl excessively! D'you suppose there's a man would with-
hold the wish to be worthy of the public's tongue, to write
things that deserve hard covers [16] and leave poetry that
fears neither fish nor spices?" [16]

Whoever you are, you whom I just now caused to take
the objector's rôle; in my poems if a thing chances to come   45
out all right—for that's once in a blue moon –if a thing,
though, comes out all right, I'd not fear being applauded –
I haven't so horny a heart. But I won't have the end and
the ideal of excellence to be your 'Bravo!' and your 'Encore!'
Search an 'Encore!' right through; what isn't there inside   50
it? –Attius's *Iliad,* drunk on hellebore! [17] All extempore
poemettes of an undigested élite! [17] All the writing from
cedar-panelled studies! [18]

15

scribitur in citreis? calidum scis ponere sumen,
scis comitem horridulum trita donare lacerna,
55 et 'verum,' inquis, 'amo, verum mihi dicite de me.'
qui pote? vis dicam? nugaris, cum tibi, calve,
pinguis aqualiculus propenso sesquipede extet.
o Iane! a tergo quem nulla ciconia pinsit
nec manus auriculas imitari mobilis albas
60 nec linguae quantum sitiat canis Apula tantae,
vos, o patricius sanguis, quos vivere fas est
occipiti caeco, posticae occurrite sannae.
"quis populi sermo est?" quis enim nisi carmina molli
nunc demum numero fluere, ut per leve severos
65 effundat iunctura unguis? 'scit tendere versum
non secus ac si oculo rubricam derigat uno.
sive opus in mores, in luxum, in prandia regum
dicere, res grandes nostro dat Musa poetae.'
ecce modo heroas sensus adferre docemus
70 nugari solitos Graece, nec ponere lucum
artifices nec rus saturum laudare 'ubi corbes
et focus et porci et fumosa Palilia feno,
unde Remus sulcoque terens dentalia, Quinti,
cum trepida ante boves dictatorem induit uxor
75 et tua aratra domum lictor tulit. "euge poeta!
est nunc Brisaei quem venosus liber Acci,
sunt quos Pacuviusque et verrucosa moretur
Antiopa aerumnis cor luctificabile fulta?"
hos pueris monitus patres infundere lippos
80 cum videas, quaerisne unde haec sartago loquendi
venerit in linguas, unde istud dedecus in quo
trossulus exultat tibi per subsellia levis?

57 *protenso* (vel *-to*) *a*, Hieron. Adv. Iov. 2.21, In Hierem.
      3.15.3. Prisc. GLK II p. 251
59 *imitata est aΦ*
60 *tantum* Wdr
61 *ius* PGWΣ (LU)
65 *versus* Bern. B.539
69 *videmus aΦΣ* (LU)
70 *lucos* r
74 *quem* aCLR Bob. *dictaturam* Φ

You've the wit to serve caviar, the wit to present an
old coat to a poor shivering dependant; then you say: 'I
love the truth. Friends, tell me truly about myself!' How   55
should they? D'you want *me* to?—You're not for real; since
you, baldy, have a fat hanging half-yard of protuberant
belly! [19]

For the love of Janus (who's pecked at by no stork, [20]
nor by hands nimbly imitative of white ears [20] nor tongues
as big as the thirst of a Kalahari dog [20])!—o privileged,   60
lordly progeny, blind at the back of your heads, run to
answer their backdoor grimaces!

"What says the Public?"

Well, what?—if not that poetry now at last has light
and rhythmic flow? Its joins [21] shrug off the relentless   65
probe [21] across their smooth finish!—'He can wiredraw a
verse like one positioning the red chalk [21] with an eye
closed; or if morality, luxury, the aristocratic banquet, need
reproof, sublime material's forthcoming to our poet from
the. Muse!' [21]

Just look—we're teaching [22] utterance of Heroic
Thoughts to persons used to toying with Greek, [22] no artists   70
at their "Description of a Grove" [22] or "Praises of Rich
Countryside", [22] with 'baskets, hearth, hay-smouldering
Palilia and pigs; [22] whence Remus and, scraping the share-
head in the furrow, thou, O Quintius, [22] when feverishly in
front of the oxen a Dictator was dressed by his wife and the
lictor took thy plough home'!   75

"Bravo! *So* poetic! Could anyone now be drawn to a
scrawny play by Lord-of-the-Buskin [23] Accius? [24] Or to
Pacuvius [24] and warty Antiope, 'her lamentatious heart by
woe oppressed'?"

When you see children steeped by their bleary [25] fathers
in oracles like this, what need to enquire the causes of this   80
fizzle-pan of language that's got on to our tongues?—or of
the enormities that make the Smart Set's polished limbs
cavort on the benches?

nilne pudet capiti non posse pericula cano
pellere quin tepidum hoc optes audire 'decenter'?
85   'fur es,' ait Pedio. Pedius quid? crimina rasis
librat in antithetis, doctas posuisse figuras
laudatur: 'bellum hoc.' hoc bellum? an, Romule, ceves?
men moveat? quippe et, cantet si naufragus, assem
protulerim? cantas, cum fracta te in trabe pictum
90   ex umero portes? verum nec nocte paratum
plorabit qui me volet incurvasse querella.
"sed numeris decor est et iunctura addita crudis."
cludere sic versum didicit 'Berecyntius Attis'
et qui 'caeruleum dirimebat Nerea delphin',
95   sic 'costam longo subduximus Appennino'.
" 'Arma virum', nonne hoc spumosum et cortice pingui
ut ramale vetus vegrandi subere coctum?"
quidnam igitur tenerum et laxa cervice legendum –
'torva Mimalloneis inplerunt cornua bombis,
100   et raptum vitulo caput ablatura superbo
Bassaris et lyncem Maenas flexura corymbis
euhion ingeminat, reparabilis adsonat echo'?
haec fierent si testiculi vena ulla paterni
viveret in nobis? summa delumbe saliva
105   hoc natat in labris et in udo est Maenas et Attis
nec pluteum caedit nec demorsos sapit unguis.
"sed quid opus teneras mordaci radere vero
auriculas? vide sis ne maiorum tibi forte
limina frigescant: sonat hic de nare canina
110   littera." per me equidem sint omnia protinus alba;

87   *laudatus* GL Bob.
91   *querellas* Bob.
93   *si* aMx *didici* P
95   *si* PaM
97   *vegrandi* Porph. ad Hor. S.i.2.129, Serv. ad Aen. xi.553, *praegrandi* libri
    et Σ
107   *verbo* PR

Aren't you ashamed you can't secure aquittal for grey
heads [26] without aspiring to hear the pale cry 'Nicely put!' ? —
'You're a thief,' they tell Pedius. [26] And Pedius? On shaved   85
antitheses he balances the charges, gaining acclaim for use
of artistic tropes: 'Beautiful, that!' That? Beautiful? — Or are
these the accents of an Establishment being buggered? Am I
supposed to be impressed? And if a shipwrecked sailor sang,
should I pull out a penny? Do you sing when yourself and
your wrecked barque hang pictured [27] on your back? To   90
bow me with its grief your crying must be genuine, not
studied in the small hours.

    "But grace and evenness have been given to crude
verses" —

That's how 'Attis Berecyntian' [28] learned finishing of
lines; 'the Dolphin' too, that 'divided blue Neptune'. That's
how 'a rib we took from lengthy Appennine'! -   95

    "*Weapons and Manhood,* [29] that's a puffy, gnarled,
fat thing, surely?—like an old stick dried out with stunted
cork." [30]

And what, then, is aesthetic and reciteable with a sway [31]
of the neck? —

       'Fierce the horns that with a Mimallonean
       Drone they filled: the Bassarid fain to tear
       And carry off the proud calf's head   100
       And Maenads fain to guide the lynx
       With berried ivy redouble the Euhian's name;
       Revival-echoes add their tone.'! [32]

If any channel of our fathers' semen still lived in us,
would there be things like this? It floats emasculated at
their lips [33] on the saliva surface; their Maenad and Attis   105
grow where it's moist [33] and never thump the couch nor
taste of bitten nails. [33]

    "Must you, though, scrub delicate ears with truths
that bite? Take care the doorways of the Great don't maybe
cool towards you. There are noises here of curled lips and
the Letter dogs can say." [34]

    The whole lot's fine forthwith for all I care, no matter!   110

nil moror. euge omnes, omnes bene, mirae eritis res.
hoc iuvat? 'hic,' inquis, 'veto quisquam faxit oletum.
pinge duos anguis: pueri, sacer est locus, extra
meiite.' discedo? secuit Lucilius urbem,
115   te Lupe, te Muci, et genuinum fregit in illis.
omne vafer vitium ridenti Flaccus amico
tangit et admissus circum praecordia ludit,
callidus excusso populum suspendere naso.
me muttire nefas? nec clam? nec cum scrobe? nusquam?
120   hic tamen infodiam. vidi, vidi ipse, libelle:
auriculas asini quis non habet? hoc ego opertum,
hoc ridere meum, tam nil, nulla tibi vendo
Iliade. audaci quicumque adflate Cratino
iratum Eupolidem praegrandi cum sene palles,
125   aspice et haec, si forte aliquid decoctius audis.
inde vaporata lector mihi ferveat aure,
non hic qui in crepidas Graiorum ludere gestit
sordidus et lusco qui possit dicere 'lusce',
sese aliquem credens Italo quod honore supinus
130   fregerit heminas Arreti aedilis iniquas,
nec qui abaco numeros et secto in pulvere metas
scit risisse vafer, multum gaudere paratus
si cynico barbam petulans nonaria vellat.
his mane edictum, post prandia Callirhoen do.

111   *omnes omnes*] *omnes etenim* CRpru
112   *hic*] *hoc* M
119   *men* ΦΣ
121   *quis non*] *Mida rex* prius a Persio scriptum, postea mutatum memorant
Σ, Vita. v. Appx. A(i) p. 97
128   *poscit* C
129   *seque* P
131   *abaci* C

'Bravo!' to everyone and, everyone, 'Hooray!' You'll be my
Ideal. Will that do? 'Nuisance on these premises prohibited,'
you say. 'Paint two Snakes! [35] Consecrated ground, my
lads: not the place for a piss!' [35] And I leave? Lucilius [36]
carved up the city – you, Lupus, and you, Mucius – and broke   115
his molars on them. Sly Flaccus [36] touches every fault in his
laughing friend and passes in to frolic round his heart,
cleverly thumbing a keen-scented snout [36] at the community.
Am I forbid a murmur? In confidence? To a hole? Not any-
where? Here's the place I'll bury it anyway: Book, I've seen,   120
seen with my own eyes – ass's ears! [37] Who's not got them?!
And my secret, my chuckle, so mere-nothing, I shouldn't swap
for any Iliad. Whoe'er you be, kindled by Cratinus's [38] audacity
that pale before the anger of Eupolis [38] and their great Com-
panion [38] of old, cast an eye here also in the search for some-   125
thing well-distilled to listen to, which will, I trust, syringe the
ear and effervesce within my reader [39] – not the sort that has
the urge to mock what Greeks wear on their feet [40] or can call
a one-eyed man 'One-eye', the vulgarian who thinks he's
someone because he's strutted in Italian dignity and once
broke up substandard pints as Deputy Mayor [40] of Arezzo;   130
not the sort either that's sly-witted enough to laugh at sums
on the abacus [41] and cones in furrowed dust [41] and readily
enjoys it much if a teasing tart [42] gives a Preacher's [42] beard
a tug. For such my prescription is: mornings, the Edict, [43]
Callirhoe [43] after lunch.

SATURA II

hunc, Macrine, diem numera meliore lapillo,
qui tibi labentis apponet candidus annos.
funde merum genio. non tu prece poscis emaci
quae nisi seductis nequeas committere divis.
5   at bona pars procerum tacita libabit acerra:
haut cuivis promptum est murmurque humilisque susurros
tollere de templis et aperto vivere voto.
"mens bona, fama, fides," haec clare et ut audiat hospes;
illa sibi introrsum et sub lingua murmurat: "o si
10   ebulliat patruus, praeclarum funus!" et "o si
sub rastro crepet argenti mihi seria dextro
Hercule! pupillumve utinam, quem proximus heres
inpello, expungam; nam et est scabiosus et acri
bile tumet. Nerio iam tertia conditur uxor."
15   haec sancte ut poscas, Tiberino in gurgite mergis
mane caput bis terque et noctem flumine purgas.
heus age, responde (minimum est quod scire laboro)
de Iove quid sentis? estne ut praeponere cures
hunc - cuinam? cuinam? vis Staio? an scilicet haeres?
20   quis potior iudex puerisve quis aptior orbis?
hoc igitur quo tu Iovis aurem inpellere temptas
dic agedum Staio. "pro Iuppiter, o bone," clamet,
"Iuppiter!" at sese non clamet Iuppiter ipse?

2   *apponit a* ΦΣ
5   *libavit* Per
14   *ducitur* Nd Serv. ad Georg. iv.256
15-16 *poscat... mergit... purgat a, merges* NW
17   *nimium* WΣ (LU) et ut vid. M
22   *clamat* pr et (statim corr.) A

SATIRE II

PRAYER AND ITS MISUSE[1]

Give it the mark of happiness,[2] Macrinus,[3] this bright
day which will set the sum of passing years beside your
name. Pour neat wine before your Guardian Spirit.[4]
  Yours is not a shopper's prayer, asking things which,
save *tête a tête,* you may not mention to God. Most of our
leaders, though, will be offering incense from confidential   5
caskets. It's not to everyone's taste to banish the mumbling
degraded whisper from our shrines and have our life's
prayers plain to see. "Righteousness! Reputation!
Estimation!" So much out loud, for the visitor's ear. To
himself beneath his breath he mutters, that other: "Grant,
I pray, that my Uncle might snuff it—what a funeral!"   10
"Grant me, by Hercules'[5] grace, the chink of hoarded cash
against my hoe, or riddance of my ward, for whose inheri-
tance I'm next, and eager. He's all mange and swollen with
dyspepsia: Nerius has buried three wives already!"[6] And,
to hallow these requests, in Tiber's flood thrice and more   15
you plunge your head at dawn, purging the night in his
waters.[7]
  Excuse me a minute; would you tell me—it's a tiny
point I'm troubled by—what your view of God is? Might
you class him, do you think, above - er – whom, now? Staius,
let's say. Naturally, you hesitate; but who could be a better
Judge, a worthier Guardian?[8] This thing, then, with which   20
you hope to bow the ear of God – just tell it to Staius: "God!"
he'd cry, "God Almighty!" And mightn't God cry "Me!"?

23

ignovisse putas quia, cum tonat, ocius ilex
25 sulpure discutitur sacro quam tuque domusque?
an quia non fibris ovium Ergennaque iubente
triste iaces lucis evitandumque bidental,
idcirco stolidam praebet tibi vellere barbam
Iuppiter? aut quidnam est qua tu mercede deorum
30 emeris auriculas? pulmone et lactibus unctis?
ecce avia aut metuens divum matertera cunis
exemit puerum frontemque atque uda labella
infami digito et lustralibus ante salivis
expiat, urentis oculos inhibere perita;
35 tunc manibus quatit et spem macram supplice voto
nunc Licini in campos, nunc Crassi mittit in aedis:
"hunc optet generum rex et regina, puellae
hunc rapiant; quidquid calcaverit hic, rosa fiat."
ast ego nutrici non mando vota. negato,
40 Iuppiter, haec illi, quamvis te albata rogarit.
poscis opem nervis corpusque fidele senectae.
esto age. sed pingues patinae tuccetaque crassa
adnuere his superos vetuere Iovemque morantur.
rem struere exoptas caeso bove Mercuriumque
45 accersis fibra: "da fortunare Penatis,
da pecus et gregibus fetum." quo, pessime, pacto,
tot tibi cum in flamma iunicum omenta liquescant?
et tamen hic extis et opimo vincere ferto
intendit: "iam crescit ager, iam crescit ovile,
50 iam dabitur, iam iam"– donec deceptus et exspes
nequiquam fundo suspiret nummus in imo.
si tibi creterras argenti incusaque pingui
auro dona feram, sudes et pectore laevo
excutiat guttas laetari praetrepidum cor.
55 hinc illud subiit, auro sacras quod ovato
perducis facies. nam "fratres inter aenos,

---

40 *rogabit* aMNR
42 *grandes* PLNWΣ, cf. Hor. S. 2.2.95
47 *in* om. Neu *flammas* aMNR, *flammis* PCes
49 *crescet* in utroque loco exhibet p

Have you His pardon because in the storm His sacred flash
shatters oaks but not yet you-and-yours? Because you're not   25
sprawled in some wood, a dreadful Relic[9] tabooed by
Deacon and sheep's liver, does that prove you're free to
give God's silly beard a pull? What price will buy the ears of
Heaven for such as you? A lung? Some slimy tripe?   30

    Look! a grandmother or pious aunt takes Baby from
his cradle. [10] First with lustral spit and phallic finger [10]
she purges his wet lips and forehead, repulsing expertly the
Eye [10] that will wither him. Then she jolts him in her arms,
and her humble prayer launches the puny Prospect towards   35
the estates of a Licinus, the mansions of a Crassus: [11] "May
kings and queens seek him for their daughters! May girls
fight over him, and where he treads may roses bloom!" I'll
have no delegating prayers to nurses! Refuse her, Jupiter,
even if she did wear white! [10]   40

    You beg strength of muscle and a frame faithful to your
dotage. A fine idea: but heaped salvers and thick garnishes
have barred God's consent, and clog his plans. To pile up
property you slay an ox and lure Mercury [12] with its liver:
"Vouchsafe to bless my house; vouchsafe me cattle and   45
young for the flocks!"— How, insect, with the bowels of all
those heifers liquefying on your fire?—Yet on he goes, our
generous friend, to gain his end by entrail and wafer:[13]
"It's bigger already, the farm is; the sheep-fold's bigger too;
I'll get what I want, you'll see, you'll see!" Till, abandoned   50
and desperate, vainly moping in the lowest depths, sits just
one penny.

    Suppose I bestowed on you wine-bowls of silver inset
with thick gold, you'd sweat as your heart bounced out the
drops from your left ribs in joyful palpitation: and this is
why you crust visages divine with golden spoils. [14] For "let   55

25

somnia pituita qui purgatissima mittunt,
praecipui sunto sitque illis aurea barba."
aurum vasa Numae Saturniaque inpulit aera
60   Vestalisque urnas et Tuscum fictile mutat –
o curvae in terris animae et caelestium inanis,
quid iuvat hoc, templis nostros inmittere mores
et bona dis ex hac scelerata ducere pulpa?
haec sibi corrupto casiam dissolvit olivo,
65   haec Calabrum coxit vitiato murice vellus,
haec bacam conchae rasisse et stringere venas
ferventis massae crudo de pulvere iussit.
peccat et haec, peccat, vitio tamen utitur. at vos
dicite, pontifices, in sancto quid facit aurum?
70   nempe hoc quod Veneri donatae a virgine pupae.
quin damus id superis, de magna quod dare lance
non possit magni Messalae lippa propago?
conpositum ius fasque animo sanctosque recessus
mentis et incoctum generoso pectus honesto.
75   haec cedo ut admoveam templis et farre litabo.

59   *expulit* f² Valentian. 410
62   *hos . . . nostris* GL
63   *dicere* n
74   *in cocto . . . generosum* Σ(LU) *honestum a*

those who send dreams least phlegm-corrupted [15] stand
supreme among their brazen neighbours: their beard shall be
all golden." Gold – it has crushed Numa's earthenware and
Saturn's bronze; it supplants the Vestal's pitcher, the   60
Tuscan's terracotta! [16] Oh earth-stooped, Heaven-empty
souls! What gain is it to let the ways of man within temple-
bounds, measuring the tastes of Deity by this corrupt
carcass? – which loves to poison oil with instilled perfume
and abuses the fish's dye in purpling Calabrian wool; which   65
bids us slit pearl from shell and strip the boiling ingot's
metal from unprocessed dust. [17] All wrong! Oh yes,
wrong: but its sin has a use! Now tell me, priests – what
business has gold at the altar [18] ? The same, does it not, as
a girl's gift to Venus, her dollies [19] ? Let us make the gods   70
an offering which the great platter of great Messala's blood-
shot progeny [20] could never furnish – a heart's blend of
Justice and Right, a mind profoundly pure, a breast pervaded
with heroic virtue! Give me these for offerings, then groats [21]   75
alone are sacrifice enough.

27

SATURA III

nempe haec adsidue. iam clarum mane fenestras
intrat et angustas extendit lumine rimas.
stertimus, indomitum quod despumare Falernum
sufficiat, quinta dum linea tangitur umbra.
5   "en, quid agis? siccas insana canicula messes
iam dudum coquit et patula pecus omne sub ulmo est,"
unus ait comitum. "verumne? itan? ocius adsit
huc aliquis. nemon?" turgescit vitrea bilis:
findor, ut Arcadiae pecuaria rudere credas.
10   iam liber et positis bicolor membrana capillis
inque manus chartae nodosaque venit harundo.
tunc querimur crassus calamo quod pendeat umor.
nigra sed infusa vanescit sepia lympha,
dilutas querimur geminet quod fistula guttas.
15   "o miser inque dies ultra miser, hucine rerum
venimus? a, cur non potius teneroque columbo
et similis regum pueris pappare minutum
poscis et iratus mammae lallare recusas?
'an tali studeam calamo?' cui verba? quid istas
20   succinis ambages? tibi luditur; effluis amens,
contemnere; sonat vitium percussa, maligne
respondet viridi non cocta fidelia limo.

---

2   *ostendit* GLΣ(MU)
9   *findar ut* b, *finditur* f² Schol. Stat. Theb. 4.45 (Cod. Paris. 8063)
       dicas αΦΣ Serv. Geo. 3.328,374 Auson. Epigr. 5.3.
12   *queritur* RW
13   *sed]quod* GLNWΣ *vanescat* αΦΣ (LU)
14   *queritur* Wr
16   *a a, at* Φ, *aut* PCMΣ(LU)
18   *iratum* Sang.

SATIRE III

EXHORTATION TO PHILOSOPHICAL STUDY

Which considers attitudes to it, excuses offered for
its neglect and the penalties that neglect incurs.
(Delivered to Persius by a Friend.[1])

This, of course, is always the way. The bright morning
enters at the shutters, its light widening the narrow chinks:
I'm snoring fit to sleep off a savage Falernian[2] hangover,
when line and shadow have five times met.[3]
    "Hey! What are you at? For hours now the Dog's mad   5
star[4] has parched the crops; the whole herd's beneath a
spreading elm." This from a friend of mine.
(SELF)   "It has? It is? . . . Slave! Quickly! What,
*no*body?" Gall,[5] glassy-green, swells inside me; I explode!
It sounds like the neighing from the stables of Arcady.[6]
    My book lies before me now, with some parchment,   10
shaved of its hair, double-coloured; also paper and a jointed
pen.[7] Next, complaints: the fluid's thick and sticks on the
nib. We add water. The black cuttle-juice goes clear. Now
more complaints—the reed's running with drop upon watery
drop.
(FRIEND)   "Poor idiot, daily worse! Is this the level   15
we're on? Why, like pigeon-chicks and little princes,[8] don't
you cry instead for your mash, and angrily repulse Nanny's
lullaby? 'How can I work with a pen like this?'—Who are
you kidding? Why this tinkling rigmarole? Fool! It's your
move: you're trickling away: how they'll laugh! The jar rings   20
false; it's raw clay, unbaked, and won't respond; wet soft

udum et molle lutum es, nunc nunc properandus et acri
fingendus sine fine rota. sed rure paterno
25   est tibi far modicum, purum et sine labe salinum
(quid metuas?) cultrixque foci secura patella.
hoc satis? an deceat pulmonem rumpere ventis
stemmate quod Tusco ramum millesime ducis
censoremve tuum vel quod trabeate salutas?
30   ad populum phaleras! ego te intus et in cute novi;
non pudet ad morem discincti vivere Nattae.
sed stupet hic vitio et fibris increvit opimum
pingue, caret culpa, nescit quid perdat, et alto
demersus summa rursus non bullit in unda.
35   magne pater divum, saevos punire tyrannos
haut alia ratione velis, cum dira libido
moverit ingenium ferventi tincta veneno:
virtutem videant intabescantque relicta.
anne magis Siculi gemuerunt aera iuvenci
40   et magis auratis pendens laquearibus ensis
purpureas subter cervices terruit, 'imus,
imus praecipites' quam si sibi dicat et intus
palleat infelix quod proxima nesciat uxor?"
      "saepe oculos, memini, tangebam parvus olivo,
45   grandia si nollem morituri verba Catonis
discere non sano multum laudanda magistro,
quae pater adductis sudans audiret amicis."
"iure; etenim id summum, quid dexter senio ferret,
scire erat in voto, damnosa canicula quantum
50   raderet, angustae collo non fallier orcae,
neu quis callidior buxum torquere flagello."
"haut tibi inexpertum curvos deprendere mores
quaeque docet sapiens bracatis inlita Medis
porticus, insomnis quibus et detonsa iuventus
55   invigilat siliquis et grandi pasta polenta."

45-6   *morituro ... Catoni dicere* PΣ, *morituro ... Catonis dicere*
L Monac. 6292

earth is what you are, to be rushed this instant and shaped
on the ceaseless, searching wheel.[9]

But 'you've grain enough at home on your estate, a
salt-pot [10] shiny and without stain – what have you to fear?   25
– and a snug salver, [10] your hearth's incumbent.' And that's
enough? Or perhaps you could puff out your chest because
you trace your pedigree a thousand stages back to Tuscan
blood, or don purple to ride past your friend the Censor? [11]
Away, to the crowd with your brasses! [11] I know you right   30
from the inside: you're not ashamed of copying a rake like
Natta. [12] But he's benumbed with vice; thick fat has swollen
on his vitals; he is unblameable, unconscious of his loss, deep-
drowned: and no more bubbles rise.

Great Father of Heaven, may this be the punishment it   35
pleases you to mete to bloody tyrants, [13] deranged by the fiery
poisons of sinister appetite: let them see, and mourn, the Virtue
they disclaimed. 'I'm falling headlong, falling!'– did the bronze
of Sicily's bull [13] more moan, did the Sword[13] hung from a gold   40
ceiling more terrify the purpled neck beneath, than thoughts like
these, and the weary inner pallor one's very wife is puzzled by?"

(SELF)   "I remember as a child I many a time put oil [14]
on my eyes, thinking I mightn't want to memorise a sublime
speech of Cato facing death [14] for my idiot-teacher to praise   45
with Father in the audience, sweating amidst a party of friends."

(FRIEND)   "Fair enough! – the value of your luck with
sixes [15] was what you most thirsted to learn; how much a luck-
less Pup [15] would sink you for; true judgement of the narrow   50
pot's neck; [15] and none must whip the whirling boxwood more
expertly!" [15]

(SELF)   "You're no amateur at picking on deviant
habits and at what the Stoa, daubed with knickerbockered
Medes, [16] teaches in its wisdom to young men shorn, sleepless
and intent, dieted on beans and coarse gruel." [16]   55

"et tibi quae Samios diduxit littera ramos
surgentem dextro monstravit limite callem:
stertis adhuc laxumque caput conpage soluta
oscitat hesternum dissutis undique malis!
60   est aliquid quo tendis et in quod derigis arcum?
an passim sequeris corvos testaque lutoque,
securus quo pes ferat, atque ex tempore vivis?
elleborum frustra, cum iam cutis aegra tumebit,
poscentis videas; venienti occurrite morbo,
65   et quid opus Cratero magnos promittere montis?
discite et, o miseri, causas cognoscite rerum:
quid sumus et quidnam victuri gignimur, ordo
quis datus, aut metae qua mollis flexus et unde,
quis modus argento, quid fas optare, quid asper
70   utile nummus habet, patriae carisque propinquis
quantum elargiri deceat, quem te deus esse
iussit et humana qua parte locatus es in re.
disce nec invideas quod multa fidelia putet
in locuplete penu, defensis pinguibus Umbris,
75   et piper et pernae, Marsi monumenta cluentis,
maenaque quod prima nondum defecerit orca.
   hic aliquis de gente hircosa centurionum
dicat: 'quod sapio satis est mihi. non ego curo
esse quod Arcesilas aerumnosique Solones
80   obstipo capite et figentes lumine terram,
murmura cum secum et rabiosa silentia rodunt
atque exporrecto trutinantur verba labello,
aegroti veteris meditantes somnia: gigni
de nihilo nihilum, in nihilum nil posse reverti.
85   hoc est quod palles? cur quis non prandeat hoc est?'
his populus ridet, multumque torosa iuventus
ingeminat tremulos naso crispante cachinnos.

56   *deduxit* PaΦΣ(L), *diducit, deducit* alii
67   *gignimus* aParis. 8071
68   *datur* aMR *quam mollis* PΦΣ(LU)
78   *satis est sapio* aΦ

(FRIEND) "You too have been shown the Upward Path
by the Samian's branching Symbol [17] and its right fork: yet
still you snore and trail unhinged a head whose jaws are all
unstitched by yesterday's yawn! Have you an end in view, a
target for your bow? Or random pot-shots, is it, with clods   60
and bricks at wild geese, and not a care for where you're
headed, living impromptu? Medicine, it's clear, is sought in
vain when disease already blisters the skin. Forestall its onset;
then what's the need to promise your specialist [18] the earth?   65
    —Learn, poor fools! Explore the secrets of our world: [19]
what we are, to what end born; our place at the start, and,
where the track turns, the line to take and the timing. In
money, learn proportion and just desire; the use for sharp
new coins; how much to lavish on your country and your   70
near and dear. Learn what God would have you be, your station
in the affairs of men!—
    Be taught! Don't sit back because the pantry's full, with
all those fetid kegs from fat Umbrian defendants, pepper and
hams from that Marsian case, and your first jar of pilchards   75
still unfinished! [20]
    But now, maybe, one of that unwashed brotherhood,
the military says: ' [21] What I know's enough for me. I don't
fancy being a miserable old Solon [21] or Arcesilas [21]—bent
head, eyes fixing the ground, all on your own munching   80
mumbles and dumb delusion, pouting a lip for weighing your
words and brooding on the fantasies of some old invalid. 'From
nothing nothing comes; returns to nothing nothing.' [21]—Is that
the cause of all the fuss? A thing to miss your dinner for, [21]   85
that?' And people find it funny; husky athletes go into gales of
tremulous giggles, their nostrils quivering.

'inspice, nescio quid trepidat mihi pectus et aegris
faucibus exsuperat gravis halitus, inspice sodes,'
90   qui dicit medico, iussus requiescere, postquam
tertia conpositas vidit nox currere venas,
de maiore domo modice sitiente lagoena
lenia loturo sibi Surrentina rogavit.
'heus bone, tu palles.' 'nihil est.' 'videas tamen istuc,
95   quidquid id est: surgit tacite tibi lutea pellis.'
'at tu deterius palles; ne sis mihi tutor.
iam pridem hunc sepeli; tu restas.' 'perge, tacebo.'
turgidus hic epulis atque albo ventre lavatur,
gutture sulpureas lente exhalante mefites.
100   sed tremor inter vina subit calidumque trientem
excutit e manibus, dentes crepuere retecti,
uncta cadunt laxis tunc pulmentaria labris.
hinc tuba, candelae, tandemque beatulus alto
conpositus lecto crassisque lutatus amomis
105   in portam rigidas calces extendit. at illum
hesterni capite induto subiere Quirites."

    "tange, miser, venas et pone in pectore dextram;
nil calet hic. summosque pedes attinge manusque;
non frigent." "visa est si forte pecunia, sive
110   candida vicini subrisit molle puella,
cor tibi rite salit? positum est algente catino
durum holus et populi cribro decussa farina:
temptemus fauces; tenero latet ulcus in ore
putre quod haut deceat plebeia radere beta.
115   alges, cum excussit membris timor albus aristas;
nunc face supposita fervescit sanguis et iram
scintillant oculi, dicisque facisque quod ipse
non sani esse hominis non sanus iuret Orestes."

93   *rogabit* W Trev. 1089
106   *externi* aGΣ
116   *iram* nuP²A²V² Vat. Pal. Lat. 1710 (ff. 16ᵛss.), *ira* cett.

'Examine me, please examine me. There's a sort of
trembling in my chest: my throat is bad and its upward
breathing labours.' So says a man to his doctor. He's   90
ordered rest; but, when a third [22] night sees the surging
steadied in his veins, he's round at a rich friend's house with
a modestly thirsty bottle to beg a bath-time tot of smooth
Sorrentine: [22]

    'I say, you're pale!' 'It's nothing.' 'Nothing or not, I
should do something about that – your skin's dead-pale and   95
quietly blistering.' [22] 'I'm not as pale as you. Don't play
the heavy father! Mine's buried long since, and that leaves
you!' 'All right; I say no more.'

    He's bathing, stuffed with food [23] and white of belly.[24]
His throat voids a steady sulphurous stench. But shudders
seize him as he drinks, and shake the warm cup [22] from his   100
grasp; the bared teeth rattle, and slimy conserves [22] dribble
from his slackened lips. After which, trumpets and tapers: [25]
laid out now upon a lofty bier and caked with gluey balm,
the Lamented points his stiffened heels doorward. [25] Fledg-   105
ling Romans, heads covered [25] now, bear him to his rest."

(SELF)   "Feel my pulse, poor fool! Lay a hand on
my heart: [26] no fever there! Feel my toes and finger-ends:
no chill either!" [27]

(FRIEND)   "If you catch sight of money, or get a coy
smile from the pretty girl next door, does your heart beat as   110
it should? You're served a chilly plate of leathery veg.; their
flour was grade C. Let's try your appetite! – A septic ulcer,
invisible to me, makes your mouth sore; you couldn't chafe it
with plebeian beet! [28] You chill when pale fear unfurls its   115
corn-crop on your limbs. And now there's a fire beneath that
boils your blood; your eyes gleam rage; Orestes, [29] prince of
the mad, would guarantee your words and deeds as lunatic!"

SATURA IV

"rem populi tractas"–barbatum haec crede magistrum
dicere, sorbitio tollit quem dira cicutae–
"quo fretus? dic hoc, magni pupille Pericli.
scilicet ingenium et rerum prudentia velox
5   ante pilos venit, dicenda tacendave calles.
ergo ubi commota fervet plebecula bile,
fert animus calidae fecisse silentia turbae
maiestate manus. quid deinde loquere? 'Quirites,
hoc puta non iustum est, illud male, rectius illud.'
10   scis etenim iustum gemina suspendere lance
ancipitis librae, rectum discernis ubi inter
curva subit vel cum fallit pede regula varo,
et potis es nigrum vitio praefigere theta.
quin tu igitur summa nequiquam pelle decorus
15   ante diem blando caudam iactare popello
desinis, Anticyras melior sorbere meracas?
quae tibi summa boni est? uncta vixisse patella
semper et adsiduo curata cuticula sole?
expecta, haut aliud respondeat haec anus. i nunc,
20   'Dinomaches ego sum,' suffla, 'sum candidus.' esto,
dum ne deterius sapiat pannucia Baucis,
cum bene discincto cantaverit ocima vernae."
     "ut nemo in sese temptat descendere, nemo,
sed praecedenti spectatur mantica tergo!
25   quaesieris 'nostin Vettidi praedia?' 'cuius?'

2   *dura* aGL
3   *hoc]* o GLΣ(LU)
5   *tacendaque* aVΦΣ
24   *praecedentis* RW

SATIRE IV

SOCRATES AND ALCIBIADES[1]

(SOCR.)   "You go about our People's business" (words
spoken, let us suppose, by the bearded Master,[2] victim of
hemlock's hellish fluid) "trusting to what? Tell me that,
Ward of the mighty Pericles.[2] Skill and experience, I see,
have come swifter than your beard. You have the arts alike   5
of speech or silence; and thus feel moved, when the riff-raff
bubbles with seething wrath, to quiet its heated multitude
grandly, with a gesture. And what to say then? 'Romans![3]
This'– say –'is wrong, that bad, the other better.' How
expertly you weigh Justice in the twin trays of a hesitant   10
scale! You can tell the Straight from flanking Deviants[4]
even with a lying rule whose foot's knock-kneed; and can
place your judgement-mark[5] blackly beside the name of
vice! So why not stop that vainly gorgeous epidermis from
flaunting its tail before due time for the mob's idolatry? A   15
strong dose of Bedlam[6] more suits your skills.
        What's your Ideal? Rich fare for life? Your person
pampered always in the sun?[7] See – that old lady wouldn't
tell you any different! Go on, puff and blow: 'I'm
Dinomache's[8] son' and 'I'm good-looking'. Well you may: 20
but no more wisely than a wrinkled Baucis[9] crying basil[9]
to a seedy slave."

(ALC.)[10]   "There's not a soul dares fathom his own
depths– they eye the bundle on the back that goes in front
of them! [11]
        'You know Vettidius's place?' you ask.   25
        'Vettidius?'

37

'dives arat Curibus quantum non miluus errat.'
'hunc ais, hunc dis iratis genioque sinistro,
qui, quandoque iugum pertusa ad compita figit,
seriolae veterem metuens deradere limum
30   ingemit 'hoc bene sit' tunicatum cum sale mordens
cepe et farratam pueris plaudentibus ollam
pannosam faecem morientis sorbet aceti?'
    "at si unctus cesses et frigas in cute solem,
est prope te ignotus cubito qui tangat et acre
35   despuat: 'hi mores! penemque arcanaque lumbi
runcantem populo marcentis pandere vulvas.
tum, cum maxillis balanatum gausape pectas,
inguinibus quare detonsus gurgulio extat?'
quinque palaestritae licet haec plantaria vellant
40   elixasque nates labefactent forcipe adunca,
non tamen ista filix ullo mansuescit aratro."
    "caedimus inque vicem praebemus crura sagittis.
vivitur hoc pacto, sic novimus." "ilia subter
caecum vulnus habes, sed lato balteus auro
45   praetegit. ut mavis, da verba et decipe nervos,
si potes." "egregium cum me vicinia dicat,
non credam?" "viso si palles, inprobe, nummo,
si facis in penem quidquid tibi venit, amarum
si puteal multa cautus vibice flagellas,
50   nequiquam populo bibulas donaveris aures.
respue quod non es; tollat sua munera Cerdo.
tecum habita; noris quam sit tibi curta supellex."

29   *veteris* aVGMR
31   *farrata . . . olla* P Monac. 6292 et 19489
33   *figas* PCLMNΣ(U)
34   *tangit* auMonac. 19489
35   *despuit* r *hi] in* CNRW
37   *tu* CLWΣ, cf. Owen CQ 6.1912.26
48   *amorum* dq Ioh. Saresb. Policrat. iii.5
51   *est* Pa et ut vid. V
52   *ut noris* aVCGR

'The rich one at Cures. His land goes further than the
eye can see.' [12]

'You mean the ill-starred, god-forsaken one? – that
seasonally elevates a yoke on a crumbling chapel, [13] then
hates to rub the crust of ages from his half-bottle? 'All the
best!' he whimpers, gnawing salt and (in their jackets!)   30
onions. A begruelled pot enraptures the men; [13] himself
downs the raggy sediment of a faded vinegar.' "

(SOCR.)   "But when you're oiled and at ease, frying
the sun on your skin, [14] there's a stranger near to nudge
you with his elbow:

'Repulsive!' he spits, cuttingly. 'Giving your prick and
backside's adytum a weeding! [15] Showing the world a   35
spongy [15] vulva! Your chin's all combed and scented plush:
how is it your windpipe [16] juts beardless at the groin?' Five
masseurs might pull the plantlings up, boil [15] your arse and
fray it with hooked pincers; yet bracken of that sort softens
never by ploughing."   40

(ALC.)   "We score a hit, then in turn we dangle our
ankles for hostile fire. [17] That's life; who said otherwise?"

(SOCR.)   "At the belly's base secretly you're wounded,
but with broad band of gold your belt [18] screens the fact.
As you wish; put up a show and fool your body – if you can."   45

(ALC.)   "When all around say how splendid I am,
shan't I believe it?"

(SOCR.)   "If, villain, you swoon away at the sight of
money; if you do the first thing that comes into your prick;
and if, with many a lash warily you ply your scourge [19] in
the harsh world of affairs: [19] what good was it to lend a
thirsting ear to all and sundry? Forswear what you're not: 50
restore the navvy's [20] tributes and inhabit your own house.
That'll show [21] you the poor state of the furniture!"

SATURA V

vatibus hic mos est, centum sibi poscere voces,
centum ora et linguas optare in carmina centum,
fabula seu maesto ponatur hianda tragoedo,
volnera seu Parthi ducentis ab inguine ferrum.
5 "quorsum haec? aut quantas robusti carminis offas
ingeris, ut par sit centeno gutture niti?
grande locuturi nebulas Helicone legunto,
si quibus aut Prognes aut si quibus olla Thyestae
fervebit saepe insulso cenanda Glyconi.
10 tu neque anhelanti, coquitur dum massa camino,
folle premis ventos nec cluso murmure raucus
nescio quid tecum grave cornicaris inepte
nec stloppo tumidas intendis rumpere buccas.
verba togae sequeris iunctura callidus acri,
15 ore teres modico, pallentis radere mores
doctus et ingenuo culpam defigere ludo.
hinc trahe quae dicis mensasque relinque Mycenis
cum capite et pedibus plebeiaque prandia noris."
non equidem hoc studeo, pullatis ut mihi nugis
20 pagina turgescat dare pondus idonea fumo.
secrete loquimur. tibi nunc hortante Camena
excutienda damus praecordia, quantaque nostrae
pars tua sit, Cornute, animae, tibi, dulcis amice,

2	*carmine* LNR
9	*inviso* P
10	*camini* P
15	*rodere* P
17	*dicas* VW, *dices* CN
19	*bullatis* Wq Valentian. 410, cit. Σ
21	*secreti* VΦΣ

SATIRE V

TO HIS MASTER CORNUTUS, ON STOIC FREEDOM
AND ON SIN AS SLAVERY[1]

In minstrelsy the practice is to arrogate a hundred
voices;[2] five-score mouths they beg and tongues five-score
for song, the piece before them being, perhaps, a play for
the sad tragedian's lips, or else the wounds of a Parthian[3]
who from his groin draws the blade[3] –
    "What d'you mean? What size are these dollops of   5
high-calorie poem you're swallowing, that you should need
twice-fifty gullets to help? They who aim at mighty speech,
they whose pot--Procne's,[4] mayhap, or Thyestes's[4]--will
boil with many a meal for tasteless Sucré,[4] must cull the
clouds on Helicon.[4] But *you're* no squeezer of wind through
bellows wheezing as the furnace heats an ingot. Never,   10
hoarse with suppressed gabble, do you crow-caw momentous
nothings fondly to yourself, or strain to burst puffed-out
cheeks–bang![5] You mirror the talk of our streets, with skill
at pointed linkage;[6] you're elegant, of unpretentious tone,   15
qualified to slice away sick habits and to pin down vice in
a sport beyond reproach. This is what to draw on for your
talk. Leave to Mycenae[7] its feasts and heads-and-feet; con-
template the snacks of common men."
    Certainly it's not my aim to let my leaves of denim
scribble bulge with what might[8] lend weight best to smoke.   20
We're talking between ourselves. To you now, at the Muse's
command, I'm giving my heart for scrutiny, happy to show
how great a portion of my being, dear Cornutus, is yours.

ostendisse iuvat. pulsa, dinoscere cautus
25 quid solidum crepet et pictae tectoria linguae.
hic ego centenas ausim deposcere fauces,
ut quantum mihi te sinuoso in pectore fixi
voce traham pura, totumque hoc verba resignent
quod latet arcana non enarrabile fibra.
30 cum primum pavido custos mihi purpura cessit
bullaque subcinctis Laribus donata pependit,
cum blandi comites totaque inpune Subura
permisit sparsisse oculos iam candidus umbo,
cumque iter ambiguum est et vitae nescius error
35 deducit trepidas ramosa in compita mentes,
me tibi supposui. teneros tu suscipis annos
Socratico, Cornute, sinu. tum fallere sollers
adposita intortos extendit regula mores
et premitur ratione animus vincique laborat
40 artificemque tuo ducit sub pollice voltum.
tecum etenim longos memini consumere soles
et tecum primas epulis decerpere noctes.
unum opus et requiem pariter disponimus ambo
atque verecunda laxamus seria mensa.
45 non equidem hoc dubites, amborum foedere certo
consentire dies et ab uno sidere duci:
nostra vel aequali suspendit tempora Libra
Parca tenax veri, seu nata fidelibus hora
dividit in Geminos concordia fata duorum,
50 Saturnumque gravem nostro Iove frangimus una:
nescio quod certe est quod me tibi temperat astrum.
mille hominum species et rerum discolor usus;
velle suum cuique est nec voto vivitur uno.

25 *fictae* G²r²
26 *hinc* Cb, *his* PVRWΣ *depromere a* Turnac. man. 2 *voces* aVΦΣ
28 *haec* C
35 *diducit* VCR, *traducit* Serv. ad Aen. 6.136
36 *seposui* aVΦΣ(LU), *seposui** *(t.* eràs.) Pp
40 *artificique* cu
51 *temperet* ep
52 post 52 fragmentum e Petropolitani F.14.1 fol. 143 ductum (Anthol. Lat.

(Knock, with a care to tell what rings solid, what's stucco   25
of a painted tongue.) And so I may require twice-fifty
throats, to meditate with unfeigned voice how largely I
have set you in the windings of my soul, and make words
unseal all this that hides incommunicable at the deep core
of me.

    I trembled when my Protector the Purple[9] first left   30
me and my pendant[9] hung dedicated to my girdled Gods.[9]
Winsome friends and my new white fold[9] let me spread my
eyes on all the Subura.[9] The route perplexes; life's witless
zigzag takes the agitated soul to its Crossway-fork.[10] Then   35
it was I made myself your child. You fostered my callow
years, Cornutus, in the arms of a Socrates. Shrewdly
deceptive, your Rule's [11] touch aligned my twisted ways.
Hemmed in by argument, my spirit strove to yield. Its face,
a master's work, was given it at your thumb. [11] For with   40
you, as I recall, I spent long days, and at feast with you I
relished the early dark. A pair, we plan a single task; and
leisure too, in partnership, relaxing over a peaceful meal.
Be sure of this: my Day and yours agree in a steady bond, [12]   45
dependent from a single Sign.[12] Truth's companion Fate
suspends our fortunes level on the Scales [12] maybe, or a
moment [12] predestined for trust shares between the
Twins [12] the coupled destinies of us two; and, with Jupiter[12]
for ally, together we dispel the threats of Saturn. [12] Some   50
star there is for sure that conforms me to you.

    Mankind has myriad types; its ways are a patchwork. [13]
Each has his own desire; their life's longings differ. One

mercibus hic Italis mutat sub sole recenti
55   rugosum piper et pallentis grana cumini,
hic satur inriguo mavult turgescere somno,
hic campo indulget, hunc alea decoquit, ille
in venerem putris; sed cum lapidosa cheragra
fregerit articulos, veteris ramalia fagi,
60   tunc crassos transisse dies lucemque palustrem
et sibi iam seri vitam ingemuere relictam.
at te nocturnis iuvat inpallescere chartis;
cultor enim iuvenum purgatas inseris aures
fruge Cleanthea. petite hinc, puerique senesque,
65   finem animo certum miserisque viatica canis –
"cras hoc fiet." idem cras fiat. "quid? quasi magnum
nempe diem donas!" sed cum lux altera venit,
iam cras hesternum consumpsimus; ecce aliud cras
egerit hos annos et semper paulum erit ultra.
70   nam quamvis prope te, quamvis temone sub uno
vertentem sese frustra sectabere canthum,
cum rota posterior curras et in axe secundo –
libertate opus est. non hac, ut quisque Velina
Publius emeruit, scabiosum tesserula far
75   possidet. heu steriles veri, quibus una Quiritem
vertigo facit! hic Dama est, non tresis agaso,
vappa lippus et in tenui farragine mendax.

    ed. Buecheler-Riese I.2. Appx. 950.8) exhibet hunc versum:
      dissimilis cunctis vox vultus vita voluntas.
    fort. cognov. schol. v. Kugler pp. 89 seqq.

57   *hi ... indulgent* LG[2]Σ(LU)
58   *putret* cit. Σ(LU) *sed] et* PaVRW
59   *fecerit* aVx
61   *miseri* c[2]Σ Ioh. Saresb. Policrat. 7.19 *vita ... relicta* P
63   *enim es**(*t* eras.) P
64   *iuvenesque senesque* GLN
65   *miserique* P
66   *fiet* PCLNΣ(LU)
73   *hac qua ut* Vat. 3259, *hac qua* Ottoburan. Ps.-Acr. ad Hor.
      Epist. 1.6.52 (Cod. Paris. 7975)
75   *quos ... quirites* C
77   *vappa et* C

trades Italian goods where suns are new for wrinkled pepper
and pale cummin-seed. [14] Another likes to swell full-fed in   55
the rills of sleep. A third luxuriates in sport. [15] Dicing
overdraws a fourth. A fifth dissolves in love; but when their
fingers crumple with arthritic [16] stone, sticks on an aged
beech, late now they lament that the days gone past were
clogged and a quagmire-light, a life unlived. Whereas the   60
nightly pleasures that pale you are your books—a seminarist
of the young, sowing Cleanthes' [17] crop into ears you have
weeded. Seek here, both young and old, a fixed aim for
your spirit and provision for your sad grey hairs!   65
    "Tomorrow."
The day after would do. [18]
    "So a day's a great concession!"
    But with every dawn that comes we've spent our
yesterday's tomorrow—here's another tomorrow emptying
out our years, always a little ahead. Just near to you
beneath the same chassis the tire turns; vainly, though,   70
you'll run in pursuit; you're the back wheel on the hinder
axle.
    Freedom's what we need; and Freedom's not what [19]
gets John Citizen, [19] when qualified, leprous corn for his
coupon [20]— how barren of truth you, who think one dizzy-   75
spell [20] is enfranchisement! Here's Dama, a tuppenny stable-
hand bleared with booze and a fraud with his watery mashes:

verterit hunc dominus, momento turbinis exit
Marcus Dama. papae! Marco spondente recusas
80   credere tu nummos? Marco sub iudice palles?
Marcus dixit, ita est. adsigna, Marce, tabellas.
haec mera libertas, hoc nobis pillea donant.
"an quisquam est alius liber, nisi ducere vitam
cui licet ut libuit? licet ut volo vivere: non sum
85   liberior Bruto?" "mendose colligis," inquit
Stoicus hic aurem mordaci lotus aceto,
"hoc reliqum accipio, 'licet' illud et 'ut volo' tolle."
"vindicta postquam meus a praetore recessi,
cur mihi non liceat, iussit quodcumque voluntas,
90   excepto siquid Masuri rubrica vetavit?"
disce, sed ira cadat naso rugosaque sanna,
dum veteres avias tibi de pulmone revello.
non praetoris erat stultis dare tenuia rerum
officia atque usum rapidae permittere vitae;
95   sambucam citius caloni aptaveris alto.
stat contra ratio et secretam garrit in aurem,
ne liceat facere id quod quis vitiabit agendo.
publica lex hominum naturaque continet hoc fas,
ut teneat vetitos inscitia debilis actus.
100   diluis elleborum, certo conpescere puncto
nescius examen? vetat hoc natura medendi.
navem si poscat sibi peronatus arator
Luciferi rudis, exclamat Melicerta perisse
frontem de rebus. tibi recto vivere talo
105   ars dedit et veris speciem dinoscere calles,

78   *temporis* aVΦ
82   *hoc] haec* aCΣ *donat* P
84   *voluit* PGLNΣ *sim* PGL
87   *haec reliqua* aVΦ *tollet* V
89   *licuit* C
90   *vetabit* r
93   *erit* aru
94   *adque* PV
96   *secreta . . . aure* h *gannit* Nhp
97   *vitiavit* PaVRW
103   *exclamet* aVΦ
105   *veri speciem* NhK Paris. 3110 Prisc. GLK II p. 433 et(?)Σ, *veri specimen* aΦ

him his owner turns about; [20] and, for going like a top, out
he comes–Mr. Marcus [20] Dama. Bravo! You've Mr. Dama's
guarantee–you can't refuse credit. No need for alarm–   80
Marcus Dama's on the jury. Marcus told me–it's the truth.
Will you witness my contract, Marcus? Real liberty, this–a
gift from Paraphernalia Ltd. [20]

    "Oh? Who's at liberty, then, but he who may live life
ad lib.? I may live as I choose: surely Brutus was more of
a slave!" [21]

    "False logic!" says yours-Stoically, [21] his ears syringed   85
with searching vinegar; "The rest I'll take: 'may' and 'as I
choose' you can keep!"

    "Now I've come from the Praetor with my rod-made [20]
independence, why mayn't I do just what my freewill
commands, save anything forbade by a paragraph of   90
Masurius?" [22]

    Listen, but let fall from your brow the puckered snarl
of anger; and I'll roust the old grandmas from your lungs.
It wasn't the Praetor's job to dispense life's subtle dutiful-
nesses to fools or grant them grasp of its tearing pace –
sooner give a lute to a lanky barrack-sweeper! Reason con-   95
fronts you and chants in your secret ear: none may do what
his doing will mar. In Nature's Common Law [23] for man it
is ordained: ignorance must understand that the thing for
bidden to its frailty is – action. [23] Do you dispense hellebore
before being taught to stop the pointer [24] at the proper   100
place? The healer's art forbids it! Suppose a ship were asked
for by a booted ploughman who didn't know the morning-
star; you'd have shouts from Melicertes [25] that only swelled
heads remained on earth. Has training given you power to
live upright? Can you tell between percept and true percept, 105

ne qua subaerato mendosum tinniat auro?
quaeque sequenda forent quaeque evitanda vicissim,
illa prius creta, mox haec carbone notasti?
es modicus voti, presso lare, dulcis amicis?
110 iam nunc adstringas, iam nunc granaria laxes,
inque luto fixum possis transcendere nummum
nec gluttu sorbere salivam Mercurialem?
'haec mea sunt, teneo,' cum vere dixeris, esto
liberque ac sapiens praetoribus ac Iove dextro.
115 sin tu, cum fueris nostrae paulo ante farinae,
pelliculam veterem retines et fronte politus
astutam vapido servas in pectore volpem,
quae dederam supra relego funemque reduco.
nil tibi concessit ratio; digitum exere, peccas,
120 et quid tam parvum est? sed nullo ture litabis,
haereat in stultis brevis ut semuncia recti.
haec miscere nefas nec, cum sis cetera fossor,
tris tantum ad numeros Satyrum moveare Bathylli.
'liber ego', unde datum hoc sumis, tot subdite rebus?
125 an dominum ignoras nisi quem vindicta relaxat?
'i, puer, et strigiles Crispini ad balnea defer,'
si increpuit, 'cessas nugator?', servitium acre
te nihil inpellit nec quicquam extrinsecus intrat
quod nervos agitet; sed si intus et in iecore aegro
130 nascuntur domini, qui tu inpunitior exis
atque hic quem ad strigilis scutica et metus egit erilis?
mane piger stertis. 'surge,' inquit Avaritia, 'eia,
surge.' negas. instat. 'surge,' inquit. 'non queo.' 'surge.'

---

110 *astringis . . . laxas (laxas* c) q
112 *glutto* aVΦΣ (LU)
116 *retinens* GL *polita* CRW
117 *in]* sub VΦΣ
118 *repeto* GLΣ(LU) *repeto . . . repono* N
123 *satyri* PΦΣ Ps.-Acr. ad Hor. Epl. 2.2.125
124 *hoc* om. Nb *sentis* aVΦΣ(LU)
125 *relaxet* G
127 *crepuit* W, *increpui* Nh
130 *quid* aRW

watchful for the one that rings faulty, bronze beneath the
gold? [26] Things you must aim for, corresponding things you
must avoid—have you marked the one white, the other,
somewhat later, black? [27] Are appetites under control?
Your dwelling prosaic? Your friendship a pleasure? Can you
now restrict, and now unchain, your granaries? Could you   110
step over a coin fast in the mud without a hasty gulp of
mercantile saliva? 'All these are my property and holding'—
when truly you can say that, be Free, be Wise, with the
Praetors' [20] blessing and God's. But if, having been of our   115
mould till recently, you still keep your old skin and beneath
the smooth brow a sly fox shelters in your shabby heart;
then what I lent you above I take back, pulling in your rope.
Reason has outlawed everything you do. Put out a finger
(What's more trivial?) and you sin. No incense ever can   120
procure for fools a meagre indwelling half-ounce of good-
ness. The two may not be mixed: a hillbilly in all else, you'd
not get as far as the first three steps of the *Faun* of
Bathyllus. [28] 'A free man I!'— who granted this assumption,
with so many things your overlords? Do you know only of
masters whom a Rod [20] casts loose? When there's a shout   125
of 'Slave! go take my tackle [29] to Crispin's bath-house.
Faster, Useless!' no pains of servitude drive you, nothing
comes from outside inside to set your sinews going. Yet if
inside the core is sick and masters breed there, do you have   130
less to bear than one driven for bath-tackle [29] by the whip
and the fear of his owner? It's morning and you're snoring
peacefully:
    'Up!' says Avarice, 'Hey, get up!'
    Your 'no' 's no answer.
    'Up!' says she.
    'Can't.'
    'Up!'

'et quid agam?' 'rogat! en saperdas advehe Ponto,
135   castoreum, stuppas, hebenum, tus, lubrica Coa.
tolle recens primus piper et sitiente camelo.
verte aliquid; iura.' 'sed Iuppiter audiat.' 'eheu,
baro, regustatum digito terebrare salinum
contentus perages, si vivere cum Iove tendis.'–
140   iam pueris pellem succinctus et oenophorum aptas–
'ocius ad navem!' nihil obstat quin trabe vasta
Aegaeum rapias, ni sollers Luxuria ante
seductum moneat: 'quo deinde, insane, ruis, quo?
quid tibi vis? calido sub pectore mascula bilis
145   intumuit quod non extinxerit urna cicutae.
tu mare transilias? tibi torta cannabe fulto
cena sit in transtro Veiientanumque rubellum
exhalet vapida laesum pice sessilis obba?
quid petis? ut nummi, quos hic quincunce modesto
150   nutrieras, peragant avidos sudore deunces?
indulge genio, carpamus dulcia, nostrum est
quod vivis, cinis et manes et fabula fies,
vive memor leti, fugit hora, hoc quod loquor inde est.'
en quid agis? duplici in diversum scinderis hamo.
155   huncine an hunc sequeris? subeas alternus oportet
ancipiti obsequio dominos, alternus oberres.
nec tu, cum obstiteris semel instantique negaris
parere imperio, 'rupi iam vincula,' dicas;
nam et luctata canis nodum abripit, et tamen illi,
160   cum fugit, a collo trahitur pars longa catenae.
'Dave, cito, hoc credas iubeo, finire dolores

134   *rogas en saperdas* PaVGLR, *rogitas en saperdam* NWhru
136   *e* GN, *ex* Le
137   *audiet* aVΦ
141   *obstet* aVCRW
143   *moveat* Vbr
145   *quam* PΦΣ(LU)
146   *tun* Φ
150   *pergant... sudare* CGMN (*pergant* aL, *sudare* W), cf. Kugler pp. 40 seq.
     avido b
158   *rumpi* GLW
161   *hoc] ut* Rf

'And do what?'

'Do what? Import Black-Sea bloaters, castor and oakum, ebony, incense and Cos's runny vintage. [30] Pick up the fresh   135
load of pepper, first in the queue before the camel's watered. Barter something and swear oaths.' [31]

'But God might hear.'

'Alas, idiot! Resign yourself to living on a shortened shoestring [32] if you want to keep His company!' (Already, shirtsleeved, you're saddling slaves with bale and bottle)   140
'Quick! All aboard!'– and you're all set to scour the Aegean in your mighty barque; unless, perhaps, resourceful Luxury first takes you on one side:

'Whither so fast, madman, whither next?' she cautions. 'Take care! at thy hot heart the manly bile [33] has swelled worse than a bucket of hemlock [33] could cure. Art thou to   145
stride the seas? Thou, on coiled hemp couched, take dinner at a cross-beam with a stumpy mug that breathes forth ruined pitch-insipid pink Veientan? [34] What's the aim? That the coins you'd nurtured here on a modest five per cent should chew sweatily through a greedy eleven? [35] Live it up! Let's   150
gather good times. Your days belong to us. [36] To ashes, ghost and rumour you shall pass. Enjoy life mindful of death. Time's flying – this that I say subtracts from it.'

What do you *do*, rent opposite ways by twin hooks? Is this or this the one you follow? Oscillant, you must tend   155
unsteadfastly towards your owners, then again go straying.

And when you've stood firm once and refused to obey their urgent command, don't say 'I now have burst my bonds' –a dog, too, struggles and snaps his tether; yet from his neck, as he runs, trails a long piece of chain: 160
'Davus, in full earnest I mean soon to end and cast off

51

praeteritos meditor' (crudum Chaerestratus unguem
adrodens ait haec). 'an siccis dedecus obstem
cognatis? an rem patriam rumore sinistro
165   limen ad obscenum frangam, dum Chrysidis udas
ebrius ante fores extincta cum face canto?'
'euge, puer, sapias, dis depellentibus agnam
percute.' 'sed censen plorabit, Dave, relicta?'
'nugaris. solea, puer, obiurgabere rubra.
170   ne trepidare velis atque artos rodere casses.
nunc ferus et violens; at, si vocet, "haut mora!" dicas.'
'quidnam igitur faciam? nec nunc, cum arcessat et ultro
supplicet, accedam?' 'si totus et integer illinc
exieras, nec nunc.' hic hic quod quaerimus, hic est,
175   non in festuca, lictor quam iactat ineptus.
ius habet ille sui, palpo quem tollit hiantem
cretata Ambitio? 'vigila et cicer ingere large
rixanti populo, nostra ut Floralia possint
aprici meminisse senes.' 'quid pulchrius?' at cum
180   Herodis venerè dies unctaque fenestra
dispositae pinguem nebulam vomuere lucernae
portantes violas rubrumque amplexa catinum
cauda natat thynni, tumet alba fidelia vino,
labra moves tacitus recutitaque sabbata palles.
185   tum nigri lemures ovoque pericula rupto;
tum grandes galli et cum sistro lusca sacerdos
incussere deos inflantis corpora, si non
praedictum ter mane caput gustaveris ali.
    dixeris haec inter varicosos centuriones,
190   continuo crassum ridet Pulfenius ingens
et centum Graecos curto centusse licetur.

162   *durum* V
163   *abrodens* Nh *hoc* GLN
168   *cessem* Σ(LU) *ploravit* P
170   *radere* Pb
171   *vocat* M *dices* V
172   *ne* CGL *arcess* (vel sim.) *-or* aVΦp
174   *exieris* Reru *ne* PGLR *tunc* GL *quem* LNRW
176   *ducit* aVΦ
179   *tum* a
186   *hinc* P
190   *pulfenius* P, alii alia

my anguish,' (says Chaerestratus,[37] nibbling his nails to the
raw). 'Must I degrade and shame my sober relatives and, with
reputation ill before a portal dissolute, consume my heritage?   165
Drunken at Chrysis' moistened [37] doors with quenchèd
torch I sing.'

    'Bravo, boy! Take my advice and slay a lamb to the
Defending Deities.' [38]

    'But won't she be in tears, Davus, on her own?'

    'That's useless! Boy, you'll be disciplined with her
scarlet slipper! Pray spare us the fuss and the gnawing at the   170
snare's constraint! Now you wildly rage; but "Here I am!"
you'd say, if she called.'

    'What *shall* I do, then? Not go, even now, when it's she
who sends the humble invitation?' [39]

    'If you're whole, intact and out of it, not even now.'

    Here it is! Here's where to look; here, not at a staff
flourished by a brainless lictor! [40]   175

    Is he master of himself who's hoisted open-mouthed
by the smarm of canvassing [41] Ambition? –

    'Come on! Load peas generously into the struggling
populace, [41] so sunny old men may recall our Fiesta!' [41]

    'And why not?' [41] – Yet, when falls the Feast of
Herod [42] and, arranged in greasy windows, lamps flower-   180
dight [42] spew muggy fog and a tunny-tail, [42] floating, en-
wraps its red casserole whilst a white jar swells with wine; [42]
then you mutely move your lips [42] in dread of the circum-
cised Sabbath. [42] Next there are black spectres and the   185
danger if an egg breaks; [43] then vast Corybants [43] or a one-
eyed priestess and her rattle, [43] who inflict gods that swell
the body unless you take, on rising, as prescribed, three
doses of garlic bulb. [43]

    Talk like this to the bandy-legged Military, and big
Pulfenius guffaws at once and, for five-score of your Greeks,   190
offers a penny apiece, less discount. [44]

SATURA VI

Admovit iam bruma foco te, Basse, Sabino,
iamne lyra et tetrico vivunt tibi pectine chordae,
mire opifex numeris veterum primordia vocum
atque marem strepitum fidis intendisse Latinae,
5   mox iuvenes agitare iocos et pollice honesto
egregius lusisse senes? mihi nunc Ligus ora
intepet hibernatque meum mare, qua latus ingens
dant scopuli et multa litus se valle receptat.
'Lunai portum, est operae, cognoscite, cives.'
10 cor iubet hoc Enni, postquam destertuit esse
Maeonides Quintus pavone ex Pythagoreo.
hic ego, securus volgi et quid praeparet auster
infelix pecori, securus et angulus ille
vicini nostro quia pinguior; et, si adeo omnes
15 ditescant orti peioribus, usque recusem
curvus ob id minui senio aut cenare sine uncto
et signum in vapida naso tetigisse lagoena.
discrepet his alius. geminos, horoscope, varo
producis genio: solis natalibus est qui

2   *et iricae* P
3   *rerum* Pr²
5   *tum* Serv. ad Aen. i.306
6   *egregius... senes* Trev. 1088/28 8º r² Paris. 9345² Vat. Reg. 1424
Cantab. Coll. S. Trin. 0.3.57, R.3.29 Berolin. Lat. Q. 2, 9, Fol. 49,
egregius (vel sim.) *... senex* PaVGL, *egregios... senes* Φ, v.CQ 29.
1979.145-8.
8   *recepit* GL
9   *cognoscere* Pbe et fort. Σ
11   *quinto* Charis. GLK I p. 98
14   *vicino* b
15   *horti* PaVG et ante ras. M
16   *senium* (fort.)Σ(LU)

SATIRE VI

WEALTH IS FOR USING[1]
A letter[1] to Caesius Bassus[2]

Has winter placed you yet by the fireside at your
Manor, animating with austere touch the lyre and its strings,
Bassus? – who with magic craftsmanship can set the incipient
phrase to ancient measures[3] in the ringing manly tone of
Latin song;[4] skilled, furthermore, to meditate youth's frolics   5
and, in light, decorous strain, those of old age.[5] I just now
am warmed by the Riviera shore; the Gulf here has taken
shelter where the cliffs present their huge side and the coast
retreats in many a cove. 'Luna's port, good citizens, you
can and must see.' So bids the wise Ennius, once he's for-   10
snored he's Homer (Q.) Esq., ex-Pythagorean Peacock.[6]
Here I am, without a care for the proletariat, or what the
scirocco, foe to flocks, is plotting; without a care if that
patch of my neighbour's is greener than mine; and, just
supposing everyone with blood unworthier grew rich, I'd   15
steadily refuse to bow myself and waste into a decline for
it, leave the dressing off my dinner or press my nose to the
seal on a stale flagon.[7] Another might disagree; twins made
by you, horoscope,[8] have natures set cornerwise.[8] One

20 tinguat holus siccum muria vafer in calice empta,
ipse sacrum inrorans p̂atinae piper; hic bona dente
grandia magnanimus peragit puer. utar ego, utar,
nec rhombos ideo libertis ponere lautus
nec tenuis sollers turdarum nosse salivas.

25 messe tenus propria vive et granaria (fas est)
emole. quid metuas? occa et seges altera in herba est.
"ast vocat officium, trabe rupta Bruttia saxa
prendit amicus inops remque omnem surdaque vota
condidit Ionio, iacet ipse in litore et una

30 ingentes de puppe dei iamque obvia mergis
costa ratis lacerae." nunc et de caespite vivo
frange aliquid, largire inopi, ne pictus oberret
caerulea in tabula. "sed cenam funeris heres
negleget iratus quod rem curtaveris; urnae

35 ossa inodora dabit, seu spirent cinnama surdum
seu ceraso peccent casiae nescire paratus:
'tune bona incolumis minuas?' " et Bestius urguet
doctores Graios: 'ita fit, postquam sapere urbi
cum pipere et palmis venit nostrum hoc maris expers—

40 fenisecae crasso vitiarunt unguine pultes.'
haec cinere ulterior metuas? at tu, meus heres,
quisquis eris, paulum a turba seductior audi.
o bone, num ignoras? missa est a Caesare laurus
insignem ob cladem Germanae pubis et aris

45 frigidus excutitur cinis ac iam postibus arma,
iam chlamydas regum, iam lutea gausapa captis
essedaque ingentesque locat Caesonia Rhenos.
dis igitur genioque ducis centum paria ob res
egregie gestas induco. quis vetat? aude.

22 *prandia* LW
23 *scombros* aVMRW *lautis* a
24 *tenuem . . . salivam* GLN *turdorum* aVCMR
26 *metuis* aVΦ
27 *at* r, *a*∗ P, *ad-* d
32 *nec* hΣ(LU)
35 *inhonora* aΣ
37 *et] sed* PNΣ
46 *victis* aCRW

man, for birthdays only, dips his plain vegetable[9] in sauce   20
he's bought – how clever! – by the cup.[9] In person, reverently,
he bedews the bowl with pepper.[9] Another chews, noble
youth, through a whole great fortune. Utilisation is my aim,
but not therefore the style to serve my tenants caviar, nor
the skill to know the subtle savours of the female thrush.
Live up to the harvest you have; grind out your granaries –   25
you're in the right, why worry? – harrow, and a fresh crop
shows.

(OBJECTOR [10])   "Nay, Duty calls! A friend in destitution,
ship shattered, clings to Calabrian rocks. His whole fortune
he's sunk, with his deadened prayers, in the ocean. He's
prostrate on the beach; beside him, huge, the gods from the
stern [11] and, resort of seabirds now, a rib of the smashed   30
craft."

(PERSIUS)   So now break a piece from your green hold-
ings; show charity to the destitute, so he's not pictured, a
wanderer, on a blue canvas. [12]

(OBJ.)   "But your heir will neglect your funeral-
feast, [13] angry because you've stunted the estate. He'll
consign your bones unperfumed [13] to the urn, incurious   35
about the cinnamon's dim breath or faulty, cherried cassia.[13]
- 'Reduce the property, would you?' " [14]

(PERS. [10])   –And Col. Beestlie [15] tilts at Grecian
education: ' . . . that's how, since this gelded [16] taste for
learning came to town with dates and pepper, farmhands
have corrupted their porridge with sticky seasonings.'– [10]   40
Would that worry you beyond cremation?
          [10] Now you, my heir, whoever you'll be, listen to me
a little further from the crowd. See here! Had you heard?
Victory-tidings from Caesar proclaim the signal ruin of the
German host. Cold ash is cleared from altars; arms for the   45
doors and cloaks for kings, yellow plush for prisoners, war
chariots and lofty monuments are up for tender from the
Palace. [17] So I'm staging a hundred pair [18] for the Gods and
the Emperor's Majesty, to mark his extraordinary feat. Who

50   vae, nisi conives; oleum artocreasque popello
       largior, an prohibes? dic clare! 'non adeo,' inquis.
       'exossatus ager iuxta est.' age, si mihi nulla
       iam reliqua ex amitis, patruelis nulla, proneptis
       nulla manet patrui, sterilis matertera vixit
55   deque avia nihilum superest, accedo Bovillas,
       clivumque ad Virbi praesto est mihi Manius heres.
       'progenies terrae?' quaere ex me quis mihi quartus
       sit pater: haut prompte, dicam tamen; adde etiam unum,
       unum etiam: terrae est iam filius et mihi ritu
60   Manius hic generis prope maior avunculus exit.
       qui prior es, cur me in decursu lampada poscis?
       sum tibi Mercurius; venio deus huc ego ut ille
       pingitur. an renuis? vis tu gaudere relictis?
       'dest aliquid summae.' minui mihi, sed tibi totum est
65   quidquid id est. ubi sit, fuge quaerere, quod mihi quondam
       legarat Tadius, neu dicta, 'pone paterna,
       fenoris accedat merces, hinc exime sumptus,
       quid relicum est?' relicum? nunc nunc inpensius ungue,
       ungue, puer, caules. mihi festa luce coquatur
70   urtica et fissa fumosum sinciput aure,
       ut tuus iste nepos olim satur anseris extis,
       cum morosa vago singultiet inguine vena,
       patriciae inmeiat volvae? mihi trama figurae
       sit reliqua, ast illi tremat omento popa venter? –
75   vende animam lucro, mercare atque excute sollers
       omne latus mundi, ne sit praestantior alter

50   *si* WeuΣ
51   *largiar* a
54   *patruis* Pb
55   *accede* aMW
60   *exstat* P
61   *poscas* PCGLN
63   *vin* aVMNRW *relictus* a
66   *repone* CRW, *oppone* hk
69   *coquetur* aVCLRWΣ(LU)
73   *matronae (immeiere)* Prob. GLK IV p. 36
76   *nec* aVCMNWΣ(M),*neu* Σ(LU)

says I can't? You dare! Turn a blind eye, or I treat the
citizens to soap and sausage rolls! [19] Any objections? Speak   50
up!

'Keep the legacy,' you say. 'A crippled estate's easily
to hand!' [20]

Well, if I've no paternal aunt or cousin or uncle's great-
granddaughter, and Mother's family's died out and *her*
mother's too, I'm off to Bovillae where, on St. Virbian's [21]   55
Hill, there's a guy who's my heir.

'Dirt like that?'

Ask me who's my sire four generations back. Takes
time, but I'll tell you. Add one further, and a further one.
You're back to dirt; and Guy there becomes some sort of
great-great uncle in my family-scheme. You're there ahead;   60
why shout for the torch before my run ends? I am your
Fairy Godmother; [22] I come hither, just like the pictures of
her – can you deny it? Kindly appreciate what's bequeathed
to you! [23]

'Some of the total's been taken.' [24]

From, and for, myself; but all for you is whatever there
is. Don't ask the whereabouts of Tadius's legacy of long   65
since, nor drill me:– 'Patrimony, so much; add interest
accruing; remove expenses; and what remains?'– Remains?
Come, waiter, come, and dress them, dress my greens [25]
the more thoroughly. Is my Sunday lunch to be nettle and
pig's-cheek, smoky and split-eared, so a wastrel like him can   70
some day fill himself with goose's insides and, when hiccups
the faddy channel of his itinerant penis, piss in a titled
vagina? Am I to be left with a fishnet of a figure while his
Friar's belly wobbles its lardy mass?

Sell your spirit for lucre! Trade, adroitly combing every   75
border of the world,

Cappadocas rigida pinguis plausisse catasta,
rem duplica. "feci; iam triplex, iam mihi quarto,
iam decies redit in rugam. depunge ubi sistam."
80 inventus, Chrysippe, tui finitor acervi.

77 *clausisse* GLk, *pavisse* aVMNR
79 *depinge* GNWΣ(LU) et post ras.C

so none shall thee outvie at slapping [26] fat Cappadocians
on a hard slave-stand! Expand your fortune twofold!

(OBJ.)   "Done! Three, fourfold it's coming in — ten
times I've creased it. [27] Put me a mark to stop at!"

(PERS.)   So ends the search, Chrysippus, for a man   80
to quantify your Heap! [28]

NOTES, Introduction

1. On this, his personal name (*praenomen*), see M. Coffey, *Roman Satire,* London, 1976, p. 235, n. 9.
2. A text of the ancient *Life,* from which most biographical details about Persius are taken or deduced, is translated below, Appx. E, with some notes. Other pieces of ancient evidence are printed by Bo, p. XXIV. See also S-H II, pp. 477-9, VE pp. 1ff.
3. See S. F. Bonner, *Education in Ancient Rome* (London, 1977), Index s.v. 'Philosophy: study of'.
4. See VE, pp. 47-102, Pohlenz, vol. I, pp. 281, 282.
5. Cf. Bonner, *Education,* pp. 87f., B. H. Warmington, *Nero, Reality and Legend* (London, 1969), pp. 26f.
6. Hor., *S.* 2.7.86ff., *C.* 3.3.7f., based on the LCL translators.
7. Translations (with text):
   Seneca, *ad Lucilium Epistulae Morales,* tr. R. M. Gummere, 3 vols., London and N.Y., 1917-25 (LCL).
   Epictetus, *The Discourses,* tr. W. A. Oldfather, 2 vols., London and N.Y., 1926-8 (LCL).
   Musonius Rufus, the Roman Socrates, by Cora E. Lutz (repr. from YCS vol. 10, 1947, available from University Microfilms, Ann Arbor, Michigan).
   On the very large subject of Stoicism there are numerous studies, most notably that of M. Pohlenz, *Die Stoa,* 2 vols., Göttingen, 1948-9 (3rd ed. 1964). The student and general reader may find of service: E. Zeller, *The Stoics, Epicureans and Sceptics,* tr. O. J. Reichel[3] (London, 1892), *A History of Eclecticism,* tr. S. F. Alleyne (London, 1883); R. D. Hicks, *Stoic and Epicurean* (London, 1911); Bertrand Russell, *History of Western Philosophy* (London, 1946), ch. *XXVIII;* A. A. Long, *Hellenistic Philosophy* (London, 1974); F. H. Sandbach, *The Stoics* (London, 1975). On Stoicism in Roman Society see S. Dill, *Roman Society from Nero to Marcus Aurelius* (London, 1925), Book III; on Stoicism in Persius, J. M. K. Martin, GR 8. 1939. 172-82.
8. Tac. *Ann.* 14. 12. 1-2.
9. Tac. *Ann.* 14. 57.5 - 59.4, and the later career of Thrasea, see H. Furneaux, ed., *The Annals of Tacitus*[2], Oxford, 1896-1907, Vol. II, index I, p. 508.
   On the Stoics and politics under the Empire see Pohlenz, Vol. I, pp. 277-90, D. R. Dudley, *The World of Tacitus,* London, 1968, pp. 58ff.: on the Stoics and Nero, Warmington, *Nero,* ch. 12, H. Furneaux, op. cit. Vol. II, pp. [80] - [85] ; a different view, R. Syme, *Tacitus,* Oxford, 1958, pp. 552-62.
10. The history and nature of the genre and its writers can be studied in: Coffey, op. cit. or U. Knoche, *Roman Satire* (tr. by S. Ramage from *Die römische Satire*[3], Göttingen, 1971), Bloomington, 1975.

The evolution of the notion 'satire' and its connection with *satura* are discussed by G. L. Hendrickson, CP 22. 1927. 46ff.

11.   For the relationship between *satura* and Greek moral philosophy, especially the long tradition, inherited by Rome from the Greek world, of popular moralising in various forms of sermon (or 'diatribe'), see indexes to Coffey, Knoche, s.v. *diatribe*, E. G. Schmidt *Diatribe u. Satire*, WZUR 15. 1966. 507-15. On Lucilius see Coffey, pp. 52, 57f., Knoche, p. 50, G. C. Fiske *Lucilius and Horace*, Madison, 1920, pp. 180ff., 230-8, 380ff., 393f., Palmer (quoting Porphyrion) on Hor. *S.* 2.3.41; on Horace, N. Rudd, *The Satires of Horace*, Cambr., 1966, chs I, VI. The title *Menippean Satires* given to a work of Varro (first cent. B.C., see Coffey ch. 8, Knoche ch. V) perhaps implies that some connection between *satura* and popular moralising could be looked for in any case. It certainly links that work with one particular writer of the diatribe-tradition. Horace (*Epl.* 2.2.60) uses the name of the sermon-writer Bion in a compendious expression referring to *satura;* see also Knoche p. 82. On Persius see VE pp. 119-70, 315-63, C. S. Dessen, *Iunctura Callidus Acri: A Study of Persius' Satires*, Urbana, 1968, Index s.v. *Sokratikoi logoi.*

12.   Polemical tone is well established in the *saturae* of Varro, who comments firmly, even strongly, upon contemporary society and sometimes upon politics, cf. Coffey pp. 159f., Knoche pp. 59-62. Horace at *S.* 1.4.1ff. and *Epl.* 2.2.60 alludes to *satura* as a hostile genre, as perhaps does Trebonius in Cicero *ad Fam.* 12.16.3. See further Coffey pp. 61f., 63f., Knoche p. 71.

13.   Especially *S.* 1.1.120f., 1.4.14-16. See also 2.7.45, 1.3.139.

14.   See Coffey pp. 98f.

15.   It is possible that the emperor and his circle would have felt themselves touched by Persius's mockery in poem 1, although there is no firm evidence that they were referred to specifically. See N. Rudd, *The Satires of Horace and Persius*, Harmondsworth, 1973, pp. 16f, Warmington, *Nero*, p. 154, also Appendix A (i) p. 97.

Poem 1 names few individuals and none are persons of influence (cf. Coffey p. 110). In poems 2 and 6 there is passing mention of persons, Cotta Messalinus and Caligula, whose time of influence lies in the past. This is a practice found in Juvenal and in a fragment of Turnus, another *satura*-writer of imperial date. United with the generalised but pointed type of criticism offered by poem 1, this practice would produce the kind of writing we should expect from an author who desired to write topical satire but was restrained by prudence. Such a manner of writing is, however, untypical of Persius's moral poetry.

16.   'Constantly with' Cornutus; admiration for Claudius Agathinus and Petronius Aristocrates; bequests to Cornutus.

17.   He is sufficiently aware of the issues in the affair of Caligula's "triumph", Sat. 6.43ff., n.17 ad loc.

18.   Compare the attitude he expresses at Sat. 5.30-5.

19. Cf. title-notes to Satt. 2, 4, 5, 6, and Satt. 3 n. 19, 4 n. 4, 5 nn. 21, 23, 26, 42
20. With S-H II, pp. 480f., Knoche p. 132ff., contrast Quint. 10.1.94, Mart. 4.29.
7f., E. W. Gosse, *The Life and Letters of John Donne* (London, 1899), Vol. I,
pp. 29-35, R. C. Bald, *John Donne, A Life* (Oxford, 1970), pp. 283f. See too
J. P. Sullivan, *Ramus* 1. 1972. 48-51.
21. J. P. Sullivan, art. cit., esp. pp. 58-61, H. Bardon, *Latomus,* 34. 1975. 319-35,
675-98.
22. The opinion of E. Marmorale, cited by H. Beikircher, *Kommentar zur VI.
Satire des A. Persius Flaccus,* Wien, 1969, pp. 14f.; note a similar comment
upon the lyric poems of Horace, H. P. Syndikus, *Die Lyrik des Horaz,*
Darmstadt, 1972, Vol. I, p. 15. H. Bardon, artt. citt., distinguishes between
those who believe that there is a connected strand of thought to which the
images contribute in a systematic way and those for whom the arrangement
of the images is less deliberate, although they still contribute to a composite
effect. In practice Beikircher belongs to the former group, and so do I.
23. Instances: ingenious and significant combinations, '(my spirit) strove to yield'
5.39, or repetitions, 1.27; violent metaphor, 'frypan of language', 1.80;
metaphors mixed, revived 'from dead', or extended. Sometimes a seemingly
concrete composite picture proceeds from the neatness and assurance with
which this is done, and the result may be disturbing: ' . . . floats emasculated
at their lips . . . grow where it's moist', 1.104f. with n. 33, Bardon art. cit.
p. 679. Metaphors may be given interesting or paradoxical connections with
the idea for which they stand, cf. 3.82, ' . . . pouting a lip (on which) to
weigh . . . words'. Cf. W. Kugler, *Des Persius Wille zu sprachlicher Gestaltung
in seiner Wirkung auf Ausdruck und Komposition,* Würzburg, 1940, pp. 4-54.
At pp. 78f. Kugler gives a careful study of the complexities of the argument
at Sat.6. 14ff. Ideas and speech-registers are briskly juxtaposed at 2.9f.,
'Grant, I pray, that . . . might snuff it', *o si/ebulliat.* Persius's dialogue con-
tains much swift and curt exchange and causes difficulties of interpretation,
as a number of the footnotes and appendices to the translation witness, cf.
Coffey p. 101. He has a tendency to begin dialogue without warning and,
where he mentions a speaker, to do so only after he has spoken (e.g.
2.8, 3.5, 6.57). For comment on an extended passage see Rudd, pp. 18f.,
Anderson loc. cit. in n. 29 below. It seems likely that 'pointed linkage' at
5.14 is a description of some or all of these features.
24. Cf. Beikircher, p. 13: "(Persius) wishes to rob the reader of the feeling of
security . . . ".
One aspect of this situation is that the *Satires* have no damaging likeness to
stereotypes of the sermon, which will have existed in abundance then as
now. No bored, indifferent or mocking response of the type which easily
greets such stereotypes (cf. 3.77ff.) is possible.
25. On Persius's intolerance of the values of society see W. S. Anderson, WZUR
15. 1966. 409-16, esp. n. 9. Cf. passages adduced by E. G. Schmidt, ibid.
pp. 511-13, Hor. *C.* 3. 2. 20, Orelli-Baiter ad loc., Sen. *Helv.* 5.6.1, *Cons.*

Sap. 13.1-3. I think Anderson somewhat mistakes the poet's own stance, cf. Sat. 5. 21-40, but esp. 115 'our mould': also Seneca on Progress, A. L. Motto, *Guide to the Thought of L. Annaeus Seneca,* Amsterdam, 1970 pp. 174f.

26. See above, n. 11. Cf. some of the sayings of Bion, Diog. Laert. 4.46ff. and the accounts of Varro's 'Satires in the manner of Menippus' (and not least their titles) in Coffey and Knoche. Abruptness in the management of dialogue is a prominent feature of Epictetus's manner.

27. Sat. 3.44ff. See S. F. Bonner, *Roman Declamation in the late Republic and early Empire* (Liverpool, 1949), W. C. Summers, ed., *Select Letters of Seneca* (London, 1932), Introduction A, B.I, III, esp. pp. xxxviiis., lxxviii - lxxx, xciv. Separation into two totally distinct sources of influence is probably unrealistic: practitioners in the two fields of activity, which had co-existed for centuries, drew freely upon each other's inventions both of style and matter, and upon a stock of literary techniques which resulted from them.

28. Bonner, *Declamation,* pp. 67-70, 165-7, Summers, pp. lxxxii-xc. Persius' dislike of Seneca is noted in the ancient *Life,* lines 24f. Bardon, art. cit. pp. 333f. calls attention to phrases in Seneca, *Ep.* 114. 10-15 which, if not directly critical of Persius, certainly represent a line of criticism which could be (and has been) advanced against him.

29. Cf. above, with nn. 21-4, Appendices A(i), A(ii), p. 107 on Sat. 1. Further see W. S. Anderson, WZUR 15. 1966. 414f.

30. Colloquial idiom was both a natural and a traditional one for *satura*-writers to use. See Coffey's Index s.v. *colloquial language,* Knoche pp. 51f., 84f., 132. The elements of Persius's diction, too, are predominantly colloquial (cf. 5.10ff.), although his method of using them differs from the easy and naturalistic one of his predecessors. He would probably have characterised the difference as a tendency to "something concentrated", 1.125. See Coffey p. 115f. and the studies of V. d'Agostino RIGI 12. 1928. (3/4). 11-32, 13. 1929. (1/2). 105-29, (3/4). 21-39, 14. 1930. (1/2). 21-40, (3/4). 75-96 and G. Faranda RIL 88. 1955. 512-38.

31. Sat. 3. 35-43 is another case in point. Cf. also Appx. A(ii) on Sat. 1, p. 107f.

32. Modern studies of Persius's Horatian allusions have been made by D. Henss, *Studien zur Imitationstechnik des Persius* (Diss., Marburg, 1951), *Die Imitationstechnik des Persius,* Philol. 99. 1955. 277-94, and by N. Rudd, *Lines of Enquiry* (Cambridge, 1976), ch. 3.

NOTES, Prologue

1. This poem is placed *after* the Satt. in MSS A and B and was originally omitted in P, but cf. C1 pp. xviiis., VE pp. 354, 356.

    P. defines his poetic vocation, relating it to mythic and metaphorical images from literary tradition which were used in talk of the (divine) inspiration or other excellence of a poet's work– the Drink, Fount, Mountain, Dream, of Inspiration; Muse's nectar (or other liquor). For the tradition and for use of catch-phrases deriving from it in literary remains, some of which are almost contemporary with P., cf. refs. of A. Kambylis, *Die Dichterweihe u. ihre Symbolik,* Heidelberg, 1965, esp. chs. III-V. Kambylis associates them all in greater or less degree with the poet Callimachus (3rd cent. B.C.) and with the Callimachean 'refined' tradition of poetry among the Greeks and Romans (cf. OCD s.v. *Alexandrianism, Latin*) exemplified, probably, by the type of composition parodied or quoted in Sat. 1, where see also Appx. A(i). W. Wimmel, *Kallimachos in Rom* (Hermes Einzelschr. 16, Wiesbaden, 1960) p. 310 notes that ' . . . (the Refined) is no longer available to Persius *as an idea opposed to the ordinary hackneyed run of poetry'* (my italics). See also S. Commager, *The Odes of Horace,* New Haven, Yale U.P., 1962, pp. 1-13. Cf. also n. 4.

    Rudd, pp. 18f., discusses P.'s use of language in this poem.

2. Hippocrene (Horse Spring) was on Mt. Helicon, home of the Muses who commissioned the early Greek poet Hesiod (*Theog.* 1-34, M. L. West on v.6). Kambylis (op. cit. pp. 73f., 98-104, 110f., 113-16, 122) surmises that Callimachus invented the notion that the Muses inspired both Hesiod and himself by giving them a drink of its water; also the myth that the Spring was created by the tread of Pegasus ('Dobbin', P.), whose name Hesiod had derived from πηγαί, 'springs' (*Theog.* 282).

    For Callimachus's Dream cf. Kamb. pp. 70-2, 90-1, 102, 104ff. For Ennius (?) on Parnassus, here referred to, at least acc. to Anc. Comm., cf. Sat. 6.10f. and n.6, O. Skutsch, *Studia Enniana* (London, 1968) pp. 7-9, 126f., but also Kamb. pp. 195-7, 201.

3. Pirene; spring at Corinth, also associated with Pegasus (Pind. *Ol.* 13.61ff.); spoken of elsewhere in extant lit. as a source of inspiration only by Statius, *Silv.* 1.4.26f., 2.7.2-4, *Theb.* 4.60-2; for general refs., PW s.v. *Peirene (3),* esp. 109.60-8.

    For literary men's *pallor* cf. Juv. 7.97, Mayor ad loc., Plin. *Ep.* 6.2.2.

    For poets' *busts* and their *ivy crowns,* Mayor on Juv. 7.29, DS s.v. *imago* p. 411a.

4. 'of Minstrelsy', lit. (e.g.) 'of the Prophets': "Prophets/Rites (of the Muses)", i.e. "poets", "poetry", are conventional expressions and sometimes clichés,

e.g. Gow on Theocr. 16.29, 22.116f., Callim. *H. Apoll.* 110 (?), Hor. *Od.* 3.1.3, Prop. 4.6.1, Ov. *Tr.* and *E.P.* passim, and esp. Mart. 7.63.3, 5, also 1.34 below; cf. Commager, op. cit. in n. 1, pp. 13-22, J. K. Newman, *Augustus and the New Poetry* (Bruxelles-Berchem, 1967) ch. IV, L. P. Wilkinson, *Gnomon* 41.1969.158.

Ovid in exile had used (*E.P.* 2.9.64, 2.10.17, 3.4.67, 4.8.78-82, cf. 2.5.71f., 4.2.49) a variant of the above idea to enlist support from fellow-poets at Rome: that they and he shared '*communal* Rites', as e.g. members of the same family were said to do (Livy 4.2.6, Cic. *Off.* 1.17.55, an important religious concept, PW s.v. *sacra* 1657.50ff.).

'Chapel', lit. (approx.): '(rural) parish' (*pagus*), cf. DS s.v. p. 276a.

5. The spurious verse (see textual apparatus) means 'who once (taught) the raven to give its hollow greeting?' It has poor and confused MS support (and makes poor sense after v.9) and would disturb the balance of these prologue-lines in which each main subject is treated in seven vv. Also 'once' (*olim*) seems superfluous. The line was perhaps inserted so that 'raven-' in v.13 could refer back to something, as does 'magpie-'.

6. For the phraseology of this line cf. Callimachus *Aet.* Prol. v. 33, A.P. 7.29.3-4, 9.230.2 (? reign of Tiberius, A.S.F. Gow, D. L. Page, *The Greek Anthology: The Garland of Philip,* Cambr., 1968, vol. II, p. 301), Kamb. pp. 85ff., 100 n. 93. See also nn. 1, 2 above.

NOTES, Satire 1.

1. A poem of 'programmatic' material, in part at least of a type traditional in Satire, announcing the poet's intentions and his attitudes to literature and to his readers, cf. L. R. Shero, *The Satirist's Apologia,* Univ. of Wisconsin Studd. in Lang. and Lit. XV, 1922, 148ff., E. J. Kenney, PCPhS 188.1962.35ff.

   For theories which associated a person's moral character with the character of his style, cf. Sen. *Ep.* 114 (Ja, CN etc.) and especially the refs. and comments of Br pp. 16-18, 23-5.

   On the literary background see Prol. with nn. 1-4,6. Several tendencies or ideals of contemporary writing which the Satire notices have similarities with those reflected in the Letters of the Younger Pliny a generation later: light verse, a smooth, flowing style (P. passim), 3.1.7, 4.14.1, 3f., 9, 4.27.1, 4f., 5.17.2, 7.4, 9.22.2: variety of tone (P. vv.63-7, 14, 51), 4.14.3, 4.27.1, 5.17.2, 9.22.2: effeminate eloquence in court (P. vv.85ff.), 2.14.12f.: admiration of older authors (P. vv. 76-8), 1.16.2f., 5f., 6.21.1f., 4, 9.22.1f.: strong or anxious regard for, and extraneous measures to achieve, favourable reaction from audiences (P. vv.2ff., 15ff., 36-42, 47-9, 84, 87), 1.13.5f., 2.14.4ff., 4.27.5, 5.3.8-10, 5.17.4f., 6.2.2: corruption of standards of truth (P. vv. 7, 48f., 55ff.) 2.14.8, 4.14.10.

   G. L. Hendrickson, CP 23.1928.102-7 would print the Satire as a dramatic monologue rather than as a dialogue.

   (Reports and discussions may be found in Appendices A(i-iii) concerning P.'s citations of contemporary literature, the interpretation of certain passages and of aspects of the imagery in this Satire.)

2. May be a quotation from Lucilius Bk. I: would recall the phraseology of Lucretius, Br p. 67, n. 1. All edd. known to me attribute the line to P. as speaker. Suggestions concerning speech-distribution in vv.1-3 are made by Ramorino (see D), G. L. Hendrickson, CP 23.1928.100, 106f., M. L. West, CR (n.s.) 11.1961.204, N. E. Collinge, CR (n.s.) 17.1967.132.

3. Hector at *Iliad* 22. 99ff. " . . . if I go within the gates *Polydamas* will be the first to heap reproach upon me . . . I dare not look Trojan men and *Trojan ladies* in the face . . . " Thence proverbially of redoubtable critics, cf. Ja quoting Cic. *Att.* 2.5.1, 7.1.4, 8.16.2.

   "Attius Labeo made a dreadful verse-translation of Homer's *Iliad* "— Anc. Comm. on v.50, cf., a.h.l., Anc. Comm. and refs. of Sciv.

4. A pointer (*examen*) mounted at right angles to the beam of a balance indicated, by its alignment with some scale or with a marker of the vertical, the movements and the point of equilibrium of the scale-pans, see DS s.v. *Libra* 1225a, M. della Corte *Mon. Ant. pubbl. per cura della Reale Accad. dei Lincei* 21.1912.9-13, 31. Illust. ibid. figg. 2.7, 3, 4, Chambers' *Encycl.,* 1973, vol. 14, 'Weights and Weighing' Pl. II. 1.

5. 'We're out of short pants', more lit. 'we've left playthings' (lit. 'nuts' cf. OLD *nux* 1.b) 'behind'.

'Heavy Father', lit. 'paternal uncles', proverbially a source of stern moral disapproval, cf. Ja, CN.

6. On oral literary performances at Rome the evidence (including the views of enthusiasts for them) is given by Mayor Juv. vol. I pp. 173-81, 289-90 (with J. D. Duff on Juv. 7.86); see also Friedländer *RLM* III 39ff. For dress on these occasions, Mayor vol. I pp. 136ff.

'sardonyx-birthstone'. I hesitatingly translate so. Josephus *A.J.* 3.186, Clem. Alex. *Strom.* 5.6 (Migne, *Patrol. Graec.* 9. col. 64) and Philo Judaeus *Questions and Answers on Exodus*, II.112-14 (with nn. of R. Marcus, LCL *Philo*, Supplement II) link months or zodiacal seasons with the twelve stones of the Jewish High Priest's breast-plate, which makes it seem at least possible that persons wore birthstones in antiquity. (For P.'s awareness and use of superstition, cf. 2.32ff., 5.180ff., with nn. For superstition concerned with audience-reaction cf. Pliny *Ep.* 6.2.2, *Orphei Lithica*, ed. E. Abel, Berlin, 1881, vv.327f. (the wearing of a magnet-stone) cf. PW s.v. *Gemmen.* 1098. 39ff.) See G. F. Kunz, *The Curious Lore of Precious Stones* (Philadelphia, London, 1913) who accepts somewhat doubtfully (pp. 308, 316ff.) earlier opinion, which seems to be the prevailing one (*Encycl. Brit.*[15] *Macrop.* 7.977d), that the wearing of birthstones developed only in modern times, but (p. 307) finds somewhat puzzling the absence of ancient testimony to it. Cf. further Philostratus, *Life of Apollonius of Tyana* 3.41, LCL vol. 1 p. 323, also Eusebius *Against the Life* etc., Ch. 22, ibid. vol. II p. 539, A. Bouché-Leclercq *L'Astrologie Grecque*, Paris, 1899, p. 316, A. J. Festugière *La Revelation d'Hermes Trismegiste*, Paris, 1944, vol. I pp. 138ff., 180-5.

The phrase otherwise gives either of two possible but not especially satisfactory meanings (cf. Anc. Comm., CN): 'the sardonyx you were given on your birthday', 'the s. you wear on birthdays'.

7. Lit. 'Tituses'. (For the use of names cf. vv.31, 87, 5.74, 6.56, 60.) It is not clear what, if any, further connotations the name has, cf. edd., including Anc. Comm., Br p. 78 and n. 1.

8. A disputed sentence, see A. E. Housman, *Classical Papers* II, p. 847f. (CQ 7. 1913.14f.), Cl's critical apparatus and N. Rudd, CR (n.s.) 20.1970. 283f.; also Br pp. 79-99. See also OLD *cutis* 1(b), 1(c), refs. of Br p. 97 and n. 1.

Other versions run (e.g.):

(1) 'dishes . . . that you, disabled by gout and dropsy, would find too much!' Cf. Madvig, Housman, Cl.

(2) (a) 'for others' ears, ears whose (flattering) attentions you'd find too much when your hide (body) is spoiled (because it is puffed-up out of shape by the flattery, cf. Hor. *S.* 2.5.96-8).' Cf. CN, VP, D, Rudd op. cit.

(b) 'for others' ears, ears . . . too much because your skin is spoiled (by old age, study or dropsy).' Cf. Anc. Comm., CN, Bo.

(3) 'for others' ears whose attentions (in their desire for sexual stimulation) you'd find too much because you've gout in the fingers and disease in

the foreskin (both caused by past sexual indulgence and causing present impotence).' Br pp. 85-90, 99, 146-8.

(1) and (3) adopt the reading *articulis*, 'fingers' (Madvig) for *auriculis*, 'ear (MSS) in v. 23.

(1) and the version in the text assume that the relative pronoun *quibus* ('that', 'whose') refers to *escas*, 'dishes'; 2(a) and (b) that it refers to *auriculis*, v.23; (3) that it refers to *auriculis* in v.22.

Others take 'old man' (*vetule*) and the refs. to old age at vv. 9, 26, 83 completely literally (cf. Madvig, Housman above) or as referring to a physical state brought on by debauchery (cf.2(b), CN on v.9); but see Rudd op. cit. pp. 282-5.

9.   Whose growing-power is mentioned e.g. by Juv.10.144-5, cf. Mayor ad loc., Anc. Comm. a.h.l., Korzeniewski, p. 397, n. 41.

10.   Lit. '(Scholarly) pallor and (elderly) seriousness.'

Some add this sentence to the Interlocutor's preceding speech: he presents evidence of the wearing work involved in writing poetry, "See our pallid cheeks and aged looks!" (Ramsay). Cf. also Prol. n. 3.

11.   Lit. ' . . . of (persons) with long hair'– conventionally a mark of schoolboys, Mart.9.29.7, 10.62.2, Ja. ' . . . among the ancients youths wore long hair up to a certain age', Anc. Comm. Further direct or more precise evidence seems lacking, but see Ja. on 2.70.

On the poetic ambition entertained by the speaker see refs. in CN, D.

12.   For the practice of reciting at banquets, cf. refs. of Br, p. 100, n. 4, Mart. 4.8.

'lavender tuxedo': a guess at the social and moral connotations of the garment (*laena*) and its colour (*hyacynthina*), cf. Ja. What the words denote physically is only a little clearer, cf. MM (569-)570; OLD, TLL s.v. *hyacinthin* Jerome *Ep.* 22.13 (Migne, *Patrol. Lat.* 22, p. 402) may be helpful on both poi but the text is disputed.

13.   On 'professionally inconsolable heroines' in poetry and on the sound of the names of these two cf. Br, p. 104 lines 8-10 and nn. 2, 3.

Also possible: 'speaks a p. line or two f. a. i. nose—Phyllises, Hypsipyles, w f. o. w. a. m.-lets filter forth the words and lays them out . . . '

14.   The clients, hangers-on, at the meal (cf. Plin. *Ep.* 2.6) are probably the people referred to by *convivae* here, cf. S. G. Owen on Ov. *Tr.* 2.359.

15.   On factors usually thought to contribute to the felicity of one dead, cf. epitaphs and other materials adduced by Ja.

16.   'hard covers', lit. 'cedar oil', an ancient book-preservative, cf. Hor. *A.P.* 332 and other refs. in Ja.

Use as shopkeepers' wrapping-materials is conventionally the fate of bad poetry, cf. Cat. 95.8 for 'fish' (*scombros*, lit. 'mackerel'), Hor. *Epl.* 2.1.269f. for 'spices' (*tus*, lit. 'incense').

17.   A most violent purgative, causing vomit or stool. It 'removes the causes' of many diseases, PNH 25.51, 54, 60, but notably madness, Hor. *S.* 2.3.82, P. Lejay ad loc., OLD s.v. *elleborosus* (cf. *New Catholic Encycl.*, N.Y., 1967,

11.946a), and clears intellectual perception in the healthy, PNH 25.51-2, cf. Gell. 17.15. 'drunk': (?) cf. Kamb. pp. 118-22 on wine-drinking and water-drinking poets.

On Attius, see n. 3.

For composing over dinner, Hor. *Epl.* 2.1.110, Petron. 55, Tac. *Ann.* 14. 16.2; cf. n. 12.

18. Lit. 'couches' (cf. n. 33) 'of citrus' (cf. PW s.v.).

19. The description of the interlocutor's gross appearance may be a plain physical insult. P. deliberately and impatiently misinterprets his request in order to show that it is a means of fishing for other than the real truth. (For deliberate misunderstanding cf. 1.87, 2.19, 5.5f., also 3.107-9; for similar themes elsewhere cf. Mart. *Epm.* 8.76 with 11.90.8, and Br p. 111 n. 1.) Understand ' . . . That's the first answer anyone would be tempted to give to such a question!' However, the Latin and Greek words for fat(ness), *pinguis, adeps,* παχύς and their cognates for some reason could be used to denote stupidity in persons to whom they were applied and coarseness in literary styles, cf. LS, OLD, L-S, also passages in Br, pp. 24, 57, Mart. 10.45.3. In this context either notion or both may well be suggested as well as or instead of the above. The apparent emphatic description of a purely *physical* grossness is striking to our minds, but that lack of wit was perhaps so regularly expressed in terms of fatness as to be further expressible by physical metaphors deriving from it is suggested by Mart. *Epm.* 2.77.2, 'You might be useful for greasing axles' (*utilis unguendis axibus esse potes*), on which see Housman, *Classical Papers* II pp. 714f. (J. Philol. 30.1907). On this interpretation *tibi* ('you', v.56) probably is emphatic and ambiguous having, beside its ordinary sense, the meaning 'your writing', corresponding to 'myself' (*me*) in the interlocutor's question; cf. *mihi* in v.4, OLD *ego* (e), *se* at Cat. 22.17.

I take *nugaris* (lit. 'you're trifling, messing about') as a comment upon the preceding speech: 'You're not for real', cf. 5.169. Others (some of whom interpret it as connoting or denoting the composition of light verse, see n. 22 below) take it as a description of the interlocutor's *activities:* (e.g.) 'You're wasting time, since . . . etc.' or 'You're wasting-time-in-writing-poetry, since . . . etc.', cf. CN; Bo, Vigil ap. D, or 'You're writing verses although . . . etc.', cf. D.

20. Janus, god of doors and gates, is safe from insults offered to him behind his back because (see illust. DS s.v., figg. 4139 etc.) he has faces at both front and rear, cf. Ov. *F.* 1.89-144, J. G. Frazer ad loc., vol. 2 pp. 95-6, 6.123.

Of the gestures alluded to, the third and second (if we may trust the Anc. Comm.'s description: ' . . . placing the thumb to the temples (and) imitating a donkey's ears with the other fingers') are still in use. The 'stork' (fingers brought together and inclined downwards like a stork's beak, Anc. Comm.—pecking, presumably—) is recorded elsewhere only in passages of Jerome deriving from this one; see edd.

Donkeys are not usually white (*albas*) in anc. authors, cf. TLL s.v. *asinus* 791.25f. Ovid, *Met.* 11.176f. mentions the white (*albentibus*) bristles inside

Midas's donkey-ears and also their mobility (cf. Galen ap. Cas.). P. may have the passage in mind, cf. v.121 n. 37.

Kalahari, lit. 'from Apulia', proverbially a dry region, Hor. *Epd.* 3.16, *S.* 1.5.78, *C.* 3.30.11.

21. 'joins . . . etc.' Contrast and compare Sen. (writing about prose) *Ep.* 114.15, " . . . some are all for abruptness . . . , deliberately disturbing anything with an even flow. They dislike *joins* that lack a jolt and regard (such style) as strong and manly. Others . . . (have a) wheedling, *light*, gliding style" (after LCL tr.). *iunctura* ('join') recurs at v.92 and probably means the way in which (at 92 the art by which) words and sentences are to be combined for the most euphonious effect, a subject discussed by Quint. *Inst.* 9.4.32-44. A different sense of the term, 5.14 (and n. 6). Cf. C. O. Brink, *Horace on Poetry : The 'Ars Poetica'* (Cambr., 1971) pp. 290, 139, Sidon. Apoll. *Ep.* 9.7.3.

'probe', lit. 'finger-nails' (*unguis*), proverbially gauges of perfection (cf. phrases quoted by Ja) because used to test the exactitude of joints in building (cf. Acro, Porph. on Hor. *S.* 1.5.32, Acro on Hor. *A.P.* 294).

'red chalk', *rubrica*, cf. 'Walls with red-cord and gavil squared', Eurip. *H.F.* 945; but the proper term for a builder's marking-cord seems to be *linea*, OLD s.v. 2(a).

The translation follows VP's and Bo's distribution of speeches. It is possible to attribute (D, Sciv.) 'What says . . . finish', or (Ja, CN, Rudd) 'Well, what? . . . Muse.', or (Cl) the whole of 'What says . . . Muse' to P. speaking ironically.

For an alternative understanding of *in mores . . . dicere*, 'morality . . . reproof' see Rudd, cf. Bo.

22. Reading *videmus* (v.69) tr. e.g. "we witness the utterance of Heroic Thoughts by persons . . . "

It is uncertain whether 'used to toying with Greek' means that these are elementary pupils (cf. v.79 and Cas. quoting Quint. *Inst.* 1.1.12f. ' . . . the principle . . . that (the pupil) should for long speak and learn only Greek, *as is done in the majority of cases',* cf. ib.1.4.1): or that they are versifiers (cf. 13ff., 32ff., 50ff. and Ja, CN etc.; *nugari* ('toy') in the sense of 'write poems', cf. OLD *nugae* 3(b)). For a list of writers of Greek epigram with Roman names, see *The Greek Anthology: The Garland of Philip*, ed. A. S. F. Gow and D. L. Page (Cambr., 1968) pp. xxi-iii, cf. xlvi.

Both the literary exercises mentioned, "Description . . . ", "Praises . . . " could have been used in schools (cf. Quint. *Inst.* 2.4.24, 3.7.27). Both are common subjects for Roman poets (Br's refs., p. 120 n. 1, Stat. *Theb.* 4.419ff.; Hor. *A.P.* 17, *Epl.* 1.10.6-23, 1.16.1-16, *V.G.* passim). 'Baskets' etc. are typical of the furniture of 'countryside' passages (cf. Juv. 11.73; Tib. 1.1.6, *V.E.* 7.49, *V.G.* 3.378; Ov. *Am.* 3.13.16).

Persius, I think, wryly produces a sample, for which at vv.75b-8 he receives popular acclaim, of "Praises of Rich Countryside" worked up according to poetic (or educational) fashion and leading, as the subject often did in fact (e.g. V.*G.* 2.136-74, 458-540, Ov. above, Prop. below), via notions of pastoral simplicity (Palilia, or Parilia, country festival of Pales, protector of farm-animals, at which it was the custom to leap over hay-bonfires, cf. Ov. *F.* 4.721-806, J. G. Frazer ad loc., Prop. 4.1.19, 4.73-8, Tib. 2.5.87-104) into the treatment of noble simplicity and heroism in ancient Rome, 'Heroic Thoughts'.

The name of Remus calls to mind his brother's name too, cf. M. Rothstein on Prop. 2.1.23.

'Quintius': L. Quin(c)tius Cincinnatus, an early Roman hero, cf. Cic. *de Sen.* §56, Lucan 10.153, in time of crisis, 458 B.C., was summoned from the plough to be Dictator, cf. Rudd, edd.

23. Lit. 'Brisaean', a cult-title of Dionysus (see Anc. Comm., PW s.v. *Brisaios*) for whose connections with tragedy and its origins see OCD[2] s.v. *Tragedy* §§ 1-8. See also D, CN.

24. Accius (Cent. 2nd-1st B.C.) and Pacuvius (Cent. 3rd-2nd B.C.) are elsewhere paired as representative writers of old Roman Tragedy, Hor. *Epl.* 2.1.56, Mart. 11.90.6, Quint. *Inst.* 10.1.97, Tac. *Dial.* 20.5, 21.7. For the stylistic habits of the latter see J. W. Duff *A Lit. History of Rome . . . the Golden Age*[3] (London, 1960) pp. 163f., the frs. in ROL II.158ff. and probable parodies in Lucilius, cf. ROL III, index s.v. 'Pacuvius'. His tragedy on Antiope (ROL II, pp. 158-71, cf. ROL III pp. 234-5) described the heroine's woes and squalor, see the story in Prop. 3.15.11ff., and was thought noteworthy by Cicero (*Fin.* 1.2.4). Further information in Ja, CN.

25. The word (*lippus*)'s connotations here are unclear. Possibly 'dim-sighted, imperceptive', cf. Hor. *S.* 1.3.25; or 'loose-tongued', because proverbially given to gossip whilst waiting at the doctor's, cf. Hor. *S.* 1.7.3; or 'half-blind with too much studying', cf. Palmer on Hor. *S.* 1.1.120; or, like 'bald(y)' above v.56, merely an insult; or, just possibly, as always elsewhere in P. (2.72, 5.77), it indicates a debauched life, cf. the links drawn between debauched taste and debauched morals here, vv.82, 87, and at v.23. See Wickham, Lejay, KH on Hor. locc. citt.

On fathers' and elders' interest and co-operation in education see 3.47, Hor. *S.* 1.6.72ff., Petron. *Sat.* 4, A. Guillemin REL 6.1928.171f. Cf. Plin. *Ep.* 5.17.4.

26. For the use of 'defenceless old age' in pleading at law cf. Cic. *Cluent.* 58, *Rabir.* 2, *Quinct.* 91, 99, *Deiot.* 2, *Cael.* 79f.

Pedius: convicted of extortion, 59 A.D., cf. D; also, however, CN, Rudd.

27. For mendicant shipwrecked mariners and the sympathy-rousing pictures with which they advertised their narrow escape cf. 6.32f., Juv. 14.301f., Mayor ad loc.

28. Here and in the next two lines and also at 99-102 P. includes either fragments or parodies of contemporary poetry. Poems about Attis and the orgiastic rites of Cybele, with which his name was connected, were part of the tradition (see Prol. n. 1) to which P. is objecting, cf. Mart. 2.86.4-5, Catullus 63 with

C. J. Fordyce's introd. 'Berecyntian', customary epithet of Cybele or her rites and appurtenances, PW s.v. *Berekyntes.*

The dolphin may come, or purport to come, from a poem about Arion (see OCD). The subject of the 'Appennine'-line is uncertain, cf. D.

All modern edns. I have seen attribute these vv. (93-5) to the Interlocutor, proud of what he quotes.

29. The first words of Vergil's *Aeneid,* often used as a substitute title for it, see Br p. 128 n.1.

30. "The bark (of the cork-tree, unless stripped) grows thick and ... suffocates it." PNH 17.234. *Vegrandi,* 'stunted', a doubtful lection, see App. Crit., C1 p.xxiv n. 3, would be used as a picturesque variant for some other word, and would include the notion 'stun*ting*', cf. Housman, *Classical Papers* II, p. 877; but also LHS p. 257. Best illustration I could find of the cork tree is in *Encycl. Brit.* [15] *Micropaedia* s.v. 'Cork-oak'. See also Coffey p. 240 n. 92

An alternative rendering might be '... like a withered old stick on a stunted cork-tree'.

Ja,CN following J.Ch.F. Meister, *Über Pers. Sat. I.92-106* (Frankfurt, 1802, not available to me) understand 'Weapons and Manhood!' as an exclamation by P.– 'Shade of Vergil!', CN p. 23, cf. 24f.; and 'that's a puffy ... thing ... etc.' as a scornful reference to the preceding examples, Attis, the Dolphin etc. This seems not an appropriate comment upon the perhaps rather modern style of those examples (see Appx. A.i). If the idea of an exclamation were retained it could perhaps be a scornful utterance of the interlocutor against the attitude P. shows by disliking the qualities of modern fashionable verse, e.g.: 'Mr. *Aeneid* himself!– a puffy ... thing that, surely ... etc.'

31. Inclining the head while speaking is condemned, probably as effeminate, by Cic. *Or.* 59 (cf. refs in Greek writings, A. Meineke, *Frag. Com. Graec.* vol. IV Berlin, 1841, pp. 611f.) and for other or for less precise reasons by Quint., Br p. 128 n.2.

32. Lines rich in names and images connected with the Bacchanalian cult: horns Mimallonean, animal-tearing, Bassarid, Maenads (cf. v.105), lynx, ivy, Euhias (Details in Ja, CN; examples of the genre Cat. 64.251-64, Ov. *A.A.* 1.525-64 a subject treated by Caesius Bassus (see Sat. 6 n.2) fr. 2M, also by Maecenas frr. 5, 6M.)

According to others (Ja, CN, Cl, Sciv.) the Interlocutor speaks these vv. According to Ja he speaks also the introductory line: 'And what ... etc.?'

33. Various phrases adduced from Greek and Latin lit. by Cas., Ja, CN, Br, D show that 'floating' and 'from the lips (only)' are proverbial metaphors for superficiality and insincerity and that 'the tongue (grows) where it's moist' was a proverb applied to the loquacious.

The antics of the poet in the throes of composition were noticed previously by Horace, *S.* 2.3.7, 1.10.71. On the couch-back (*pluteus*) and on the couch as the place for study see MM p. 724, Becker's *Gallus* p. 291, cf. vv.52f., n. 18.

74

34. r-r-r-r-r (seemingly an allusion to Lucilius, cf. Marx frr. 2,377-8, ROL III vv.3-4, 389-90). It is disputed whether the growling is the mad-dog sound of the affronted Great within their thresholds, or is the snarling of the satirist against their tastes in literary composition (whence their coolness), see W. S. Anderson CQ 8.1958.195-7, Br pp. 151f.

35. On interdictions against defilement of tombs, honorific statues and other areas; and on their use of snake-pictures representing the Spirit (Genius) of the place, see Ja, VP.

   Many (Buecheler, D, Cl, Sciv., Bo) punctuate 'Paint two snakes' as an instruction of P. to the Interlocutor; others (Ja, CN) attribute 'Paint two ... piss!' all to P.; all whom I know of would regard *discedo* ('And I leave?') as a statement, 'I leave'. For the question, whether as a challenge or asking for advice, cf. 5.155, Q. Curt. 5.5.15, Enn. *Scen.* 225 V^3, Hor. *Epl.* 1.2.33, Pl. *Amph.* 391, Ter. *Andr.* 921, Ov. *Am.* 1.2.9, Juv. 4.130.

36. Lucilius: first major author of Satire, see OCD, Coffey ch. 4.

   On Horace (Q. Horatius *Flaccus*), see N. Rudd, *The Satires of Horace* (Cambr., 1966) esp. chs. I, VI, S. Commager, *The Odes of Horace* (Yale, 1962) pp. 103-9, R. H. Brower, *Alexander Pope: The Poetry of Allusion* (Oxford, 1959) ch. VI.

   'keen-scented snout': lit. 'unblocked (apparently by the coarsest method, cf. Quint. *Inst.* 11.3.80) nose'. For the (?) colloquial and allusive images cf. PNH 11.158, Hor. *S.* 1.6.5, 2.8.64, 'nose' to symbolise mockery, also at vv.40f., 109 (where I tr. differently); Hor. *S.* 1.4.8, TLL s.v. *mucosus*, Lucian *Alex.* 20, the blocked or clear nose symbolising dull-wittedness or its opposite.

37. The punishment of King Midas for inept aesthetic judgement, cf. Ovid, *Met.* 11.146ff.

38. Cr., Eup. and Aristophanes ('Companion') are representative figures of Athenian Old Comedy (cf. Hor. *S.* 1.4.1, Vell. 1.16.3, Quint. *Inst.* 10.1.66) on whose reputation see refs. of Ja, also Hor. *S.* 1.4.3-5, KH ad loc.

   'pale (with hard study) at E.'s anger' (Ja, CN, Sciv., Br); or 'grow pale with E.'s own anger' (D, cf. CN) are suggested alternatives to 'pale before ... ', cf. Bo.

   Opinions differ also about whether *sene* attributes ancientness ('of old', cf. CN, Sciv.) to Aristoph., or long life (Ja). Cf. Wickham, KH on Hor. *S.* 2.1.34, *Epl.* 2.1.56.

39. P. writes (e.g.) "something *boiled down* (i.e. concentrated) . . . *foment* the ear (cf. Cels. 6.7.7, LS s.v. *vaporo, vaporatio;* also 5.86) . . . *boil* within". *adflate* above (lit. 'breathed upon', sts. 'inspired') not uncommonly has connotations of scorching; OLD *afflo,* 5; hence 'kindled'.

40. 'What Greeks . . . feet', lit. 'the sandals' (*crepidae*, a Greek word, cf. OLD) 'of the Greeks'.

   For the types of scoffer here and in what follows cf. 3.77ff., 5.189ff., 6.37ff.

   'Deputy Mayor'; lit. 'Aedile', for whose powers see PW s.v. *aedilis* 460.27-51, 461.53-463.20, esp. 462.21-6; also Mayor on Juv. 10.101-2, 102, Ja.

41. *Abacus* (cf. Cas.,D, DS s.v. II, Polyb. 5.26.13, Alexis ap. Athenaeus 117e) a&
     dust are basic tools of arithmetical calculation and geometrical demonstratic
     respectively. Some, however, believe that both words refer to the same thin&
     an abacus in the sense of a dust-table, upon which both operations are
     envisaged as being carried out (Ja, CN, Sciv., Bo), cf. DS s.v. I, and some of
     the refs. of Pease on Cic. *N.D.* 2.48, q.v. in general; also T. L. Heath, *A
     History of Greek Mathematics* (Oxford, 1921) vol. I pp. 46-51.
42. 'tart' (*nonaria*, not found elsewhere in literature): so the Anc. Comm. (cf.
     Schol. Juv. 6.117): "(prostitutes) used to stand their pitch from the ninth
     (*nona*) hour so that the young should not neglect their morning military
     exercises . . . " From Plut. *Camillus* 33.6f.: "(At the festival of the Nones,
     nonae, of July) . . . servant-girls go around brightly dressed, making mock of
     those they meet." the equally possible but less useable translation 'Nones-
     girl' is suggested (F. D. Morice, CR 4.1890.230, cf. PW s.v. *Nonae Caprotina&*
     Rudd).

         'Preacher', lit. 'Cynic'. For the influence of Cynicism in P.'s day see
     D. R. Dudley *A Hist. of Cynicism* (London, 1937) pp. 187-98. For the bear
     as distinguishing Cynics and philosophers in general cf. [Lucian] *The Cynic,*
     1, Mayor, Juv. 14.12, PW s.v. *Bart* 32.5-18, and ctr. Becker *Gallus* p. 428,
     PW art. cit. 32.41-33.58. Justifications for it, Epict. *Diss.* 1.16.9ff., [Lucian
     cit. passim. See also Quint. *Inst.* 12.3.12, Austin ad loc. (with which contras
     P. 3.44ff.).
43. The identity and connotations of both things are obscure. If (Nem., Br, cf.
     Ja) the E. is the Praetor's Edict (for which see PW s.v. *edictum,* F. de Zulue&
     The Institutes of Gaius, Oxford, 1953, pt. II pp. 18f., Buckland TBORL³
     pp. 8-11), the body of law displayed on the white board (*album*) in the
     Forum (cf. PW art. cit. 1941.27-35), Quint. *Inst.* 12.3.11 and Sen. *Ep.* 48.1&
     117.30 probably impute an appetite for routine jargon, pettifogging minutiæ
     and prolixity to those who involve themselves with it, cf. Gaius *Inst.* 4.46,
     Cic. *Pro Mur.* 23, 25ff., Ov. *Am.* 1.15.5; and mention of 'mornings' (as
     opposed to afternoons, cf. Mart. 4.8, Hor. *Sat.* 1.6.119-21, 125-8, 2.6.20-7,
     cf. *Epl.* 1.6.20) might suggest that the reference is to working-hours occupa-
     tions of men of affairs rather than the casual reading of idlers (Ja); cf.
     perhaps the comment of Horace, *A.P.* 330-2 on the relationship between the
     Romans' concern with business and defects in their literature. However, oth&
     possibilities are: (i) some other, more particular edict of a magistrate (cf.
     Anc. Comm.), (ii) an advertisement for a play or for games, perhaps a specia&
     case of (i), cf. Ja, who interprets Sen. *Ep.* 117.30 (above) in this sense.

         Callirrhoe is perhaps a poem with a mythical heroine (see Bo, W. Smith,
     ed., *Dict. of Gk. and Rn. Biog. and Mythol.,* London, 1870, PW s.v. *Kalli* -)
     like those mentioned in v. 34 (CN, cf. Anc. Comm., Br). Others suggest it is
     the name of a prostitute (Cas., Ja) or actress or tragedy or comedy (Anc.
     Comm.) or mime (cf. Br).

NOTES, Satire 2

1. The topic is common in moral discussion, cf. ps.-Plato *Alcibiades* II, Lucian *The Ship,* Seneca *Ep.* 10.4-5 and other refs. of Mayor on Juv. *Sat.* 10 (q.v. also), vol. II pp. 64, 156f.
   For the dedication to a friend on his birthday cf. OCD s.v. *Genethliacon,* also CN.

2. Lit. 'Mark it with a stone of the better sort'. Latin-speakers use 'white', 'black' commonly as equivalents for 'good', 'propitious' and their opposites, cf. OLD *albus* 7, *niger* 8, 9. A story, probably apocryphal, told how the Thracians set aside a stone for every day of their lives, white or black according as its luck was good or bad (see PNH 7.131f.). For poets' use of phrases connected with this story and perhaps giving rise to it (cf. KH on Hor. *S.* 2.3.247) see Wickham on Hor. *C.* 1.36.10.

3. 'Plotius . . . Macrinus, a man of learning with a paternal affection for the author. He had studied at the house of Servilius' (see Persius's ancient *Life*) 'and had sold Persius some ground at reduced cost'. (Anc. Comm. We have no further information.)

4. Lit. 'Genius', cf. DS, J. G. Frazer on Ov. *F.,* Index II, s.v., Dziatsko-Hauler on Ter. *Phorm.* 44.

5. Besought by Romans, and rewarded with tithes, as guardian of treasure and giver of gain. See W. Ramsay's n. on Plautus *Mostellaria* 4.3.45, L. R. Farnell, *Greek Hero Cults* (Oxford, 1921) p. 153, W. Warde Fowler, *The Roman Festivals* (London, 1899) pp. 193-7.

6. A persuasive parallel case, in which Heaven has provided death for the benefit of the living. The husband inherited his dead wife's personal dowry plus the dowry provided by her father, if *he* were already dead, cf. Ulpian, *Lib. Sing. Reg.* 6.4-5; also Martial's imitation of this line, 10.43. Nerius is probably a name derived from Horace (*S.* 2.3.69).

7. Self-purification before prayer is usual: and especially necessary in the mornings to offset pollutions incurred by dreaming and sexual activity. See Ja, D.

8. i.e. than God (ironical. P. pretends he has to argue the point seriously for his opponent's enlightenment). Staius is doubtfully identified with Staienus, a corrupt judge of Cicero's day; Cic. *pro Clu.* 24.65 ff.

9. 'relic', lit. *bidental*: tabooed spot where lightning has struck. Traces of the event are gathered, buried with sacrifice and insulated with a low cylindrical construction (see Pease on Cic. *De Div.* 1.33, illus. in DS s.v.). The practice is thought of as particularly Etruscan (cf. Anc. Comm., Lucan 8.864) and Ergenna ('Deacon') has a distinctively Etruscan name (cf. Porsenna) which marks him as the officiating priest.

10. Possibly a "christening" scene. Babies were purified from the ritual pollutions of birth shortly after the event (see Festus s.v. *lustrici dies*). Children are especially vulnerable to magic, cf. Plut. *Symp.* 5.7.1,680D; an elderly relation, dressed in white for the occasion (*albata* 40, cf. refs. of Bo), performs an

apotropaic ritual. Possible defences against the much-feared Evil Eye (*urentis oculos,* 34) included the use of something obscene (the middle finger as phallus) and of saliva, cf. Petron. *Sat.* 131. See Ja, PW s.v. *fascinum,* P. Walcot, *Envy and the Greeks,* Warminster, 1978, ch. 7.

11. Twin types of wealth mentioned also by Seneca, *Ep.* 119.9. Licinus, freedman administrator of Julius Caesar and Augustus (see Mayor on Juv. *Sat.* 1.109); M. Licinius Crassus, the triumvir, cf. Cic. *Fin.* 3.75.

12. God of trade and profit, cf. 5.112, Anc. Comm. ad loc., 6.62 and n. 22, Pl. *Amph.* 1-7, 12, Hor. *S.* 2.3.68, Ov. *F.* 5.671-92; also of flocks. See Ja.

13. Latin *fertum* or *ferctum,* a kind of cake, used particularly for religious sacrifice (Ja, from Festus s.v.).

14. For gilding on statues cf. Juv. *Sat.* 13.151-2.

15. Possibly (i) truly prophetic dreams (cf. Cic. *Div.* 2.129-30, 1.60-2, Sat.1, n. 3 fin., PW s.v. *incubatio*) or (ii) dreams uncorrupted by wrongful secretions of the bodily humours (cf. "Hippocrates", *Regimen* IV *(Dreams),* esp. ch. 89 init. et fin.) and therefore happily indicative of good health.

16. Earthenware (often, like rituals, of Tuscan origin, Mart. 14.98) was the material of religious statues (Propertius 4.1.5) and vessels in the days of Roman religion's oldest and most august institutions, reportedly given by King Numa (cf. Cic. *N.D.* 3.17.43, Ov. *F.* 3.14, cf. MM pp. 640, 653).

    Saturn's bronze: ? ritual utensils: obscure, see Ja, CN.

17. To which ore is ground before smelting, PNH 33.69.

18. Latin *in sancto.* The noun is unique in Classical Latin as we have it. Interpretations vary: 'in the case of a god', 'in an offering', 'in a temple'.

19. cf. A.P. 6.280 (Ja). Girls dedicate the toys and dolls of childhood upon arrival at marriageable age, cf. Blümner p. 308.

20. According to Persius' Anc. Comm., L. Aurelius Cotta Messalinus, degenerate second son of M. Valerius Messala Corvinus, distinguished soldier and politician cf. Tac. *Ann.* 6.7.1, PNH 10.52.

21. Lit. wheat, main ingredient of *mola salsa,* proverbially the poor man's mite, e.g. PNH *Praef.* 11.

NOTES, Satire 3

1. On this term (*comes,* cf. v.7) see Ja p. 144, VP p. 73. For the various interpretations which endeavour to answer problems posed by this Satire, see Appx. B.
2. A noted and potent vintage from Campania, cf. PNH 14.62f., Hor. *S.* 2.4.24, *C.*1.27.10 etc.
3. Lit. a hypallage: "the line is touched by the fifth shadow". The sundial marks the fifth hour; say eleven o'clock (see Balsdon pp. 16-19). Time for lunch and relaxation after morning work (cf. Auson. *Ephem.* 6.1-2, Mart. 4.8.3-4).
4. The rising of the constellation Canis Major or of its brightest star Sirius (either of which may be called *Canicula*) was from very ancient times thought of as initiating, and sometimes as causing (cf. Isid. *Orig.* 3.71.14) the year's intensest heat and threat of disease, cf. Hom. *Il.* 22.26ff., cf. also Colum. 2.20.1. The beginning of this period (reckoned as lasting thirty days by PNH 8.152) is variously dated through the last part of July, according to the author's latitude, the accuracy of his information and the heavenly body referred to. The choice of adjective here as elsewhere is influenced by a widespread belief (cf. PNH 2.107) in a link between the dog-star and hydrophobia in dogs. See PW s.v. *Sirius.*
5. *bilis*: 'i.e. anger', Anc. Comm. A common and very ancient use of this word, and of its Greek counterparts χόλος and χολή, which must reflect a folkbelief about the causes or accompaniments of outward behaviour (later adopted as part of humoral theory of medicine and science), cf. W. Müri, *Mus. Helv.* 10.1953.35-6, PNH 11.193, Sen. *de Ira* 3.9.4, and also the interesting and readable chapter in H. E. Sigerist, *A History of Medicine,* Vol. II (N.Y., 1961) pp. 317ff., esp. 323f.
    vitrea, 'glassy', perhaps indicates greenish translucence, cf. Celsus 7.18.6 *bilem . . . viridem.* It is usually said that P. is translating ὑαλοειδής, a word that occurs as a descriptive term in Greek medical writers. I have failed to trace Casaubon's reference to its occurrence in combination with χολή.
6. Famous for its donkeys.
7. Tools of study. A study-text; parchment, probably for roughwork (Quint. *Inst.* 10.3.31, Mart. 14.7), the shorn hair-side darker in colour than the fleshside; papyrus, finely dressed (PNH 13.71-83) but intolerant of erasure, for a final version; a pen of sharpened reed (cf. *harundo* 11, *calamus* 12, 19), hence 'jointed'; and cuttlefish ink (possibly a metaphor only: with Auson. *Epl.* 14.76f., 15. 54 and *Encycl. Brit.* [15], *Microp.* s.v. *Cuttlefish* contrast PNH 35.43, Vitruv. 7.10.2).
8. A byword for the spoilt, cf. Hor. *C.* 2.18.32-4, Dio Chrys. *Or.* 45.6.
9. A technical metaphor of great frequency in ancient moral discourse, see refs. in Ja; cf. Isaiah 64.8, S. Paul, *Romans* 9.20-1.
10. I.e. a modest 'old-Roman' competence. Salt-pot and salver, *salinum* (see PW, DS s.v.) and *patella* (see DS s.v., Frazer on Ov. *F.,* vol. II p. 480), of

silver preferably, are especially associated with domestic religion and redolent of the emotions of home, the family table and stability. Cleanliness of the *salinum* is a point of domestic pride, cf. Cat. 23.19.

11. Indications of birth and rank. Persius's Tuscan ancestry offers links with Rome's early history (cf. Hor. *C.* 3.29.1) and his status as knight honours him with a place in a small-town Knights' Parade (*transvectio,* see Dion. Hal. *Ant. Rom.* 6.13, PW s.v., Lily R. Taylor JRS 14.1924.169) at which he has social or family ties with the inspecting magistrate (*censorem tuum,* cf. Sen. *Suas.* 6.1, *tuos consules).* For this ceremony knights wore a short purple cloak with stripes (or a border?) of scarlet (Dion. Hal. loc. cit.). This was their particular pattern of a Roman ceremonial garment called *trabea (trabeate* 29, cf. PW, DS (with illust.) s.v.). Though it was official dress for others too, the *trabea* was thought of as the mark of knights in particular (Mart. 5.41.5). For the *trabea* and for 'brasses' (*phaleras,* 30) cf. also OCD[2] s.v. *equites,* §1.

12. Possibly a character from Horatian satire (1.6.124); possibly an unknown or imaginary member of the gens Pinaria, see PW s.v. *Pinarius.*

13. For tyrants as symbols in ancient moral discourse cf. Hor. *Epl.* 1.16.73ff., *C.* 3.3.3, KH ad locc. The two 'terrors' mentioned are famous tortures devised by tyrants, which suggest themselves as appropriate for that reason: 'Sicily's bronze bull', in which Phalaris of Agrigentum (C.6 B.C.) roasted his victims, and the 'Sword of Damocles', suspended by a hair over a courtier's head by order of Dionysius I of Syracuse. See PW s.v. *Phalaris, Damokles.*

14. There appears to be no satisfactory ancient record elsewhere of olive oil as a treatment for the eyes; but various oils were used with other substances in eye-salves, PNH 23.76-92, cf. Celsus 6.6.6, 15, 32 with 34, Hor. *Epl.* 1.1.29, and one undergoing such treatments was expected to be dim-sighted (Hor. *S.* 1.3.25). Their simulation would give a boy excuse to miss reading-study, in this case the memorisation of a declamation-exercise, an imaginary piece written for the younger Cato (cf. Sen. *Ep.* 95.69ff., Lucan *De Bello Civ.* passim) to speak before his noted suicide in 46 B.C. For these 'suasoriae' cf. Juv. *Sat.* 7.161-4; samples in the collection of the Elder Seneca. See also Quint. *Inst.* 2.4.16, 2.7.1 for these semi-public 'occasions' at schools and the harm they do. Persius' father was dead at the time he describes (see *Life,* Appx. E). This may be illustrative fiction or an abbreviated reference to his stepfather.

15. In dicing the best and worst throws with *tesserae* were, respectively, three sixes and three ones (called *canis, canicula,* 'pup', 49). In the second game players compete at throwing nuts or dice into the 'narrow pot's neck'. The third is whip-and-top, described with a poetic glance at Vergil's *volubile buxum (Aen.* 7.382). See Ja.

16. The Stoa Poikile (Coloured Portico), where Zeno, founder of the Stoic school, taught at Athens, was decorated with murals by Polygnotus, one of which portrayed the Battle of Marathon (Diog. Laert. 7.5, Paus. 1.15 with nn. of J. G. Frazer, vol. II p. 132-7) against the Medes in their (barbaric) trousers.

It was a mark of simplicity and independence in Stoic disciples to cut the hair short and to adopt a plain diet: *siliquae* and *polenta* ('beans', 'gruel') are proverbial fare for plain living and high thinking, Sen. *Ep.* 110.18, 45.11; Hor. *Epl.* 2.1.123, Juv. *Sat.* 11.58. Cf. the recipe at PNH 18.72-4.

17.   A parable attributed to Pythagoras (of Samos) likened the choice between the steep, narrow way of Virtue and the broad, easy one of Vice to the Greek letter Y (formed, e.g. Y , Y, Y; F. G. Kenyon, *Palaeog. of Gk. Papyri*, Oxford, 1899, Appendix I, E. Maunde Thompson, *Intro. to Gk. and Lat. Palaeography*, Oxford, 1912, p.144), cf. Isid. *Orig.* 1.3.7-8, *Anth. Lat.* I.2.632, Ja, also 5.35 and n.10.

18.   Lit. 'Craterus', a Horatian name (*S.* 2.3.161); and an important one in the medical world of Cicero's time (cf. *ad Att.* 12.13.1, 14.4). The condition mentioned is oedema, dropsy, for which black hellebore (v.63) was prescribed (PNH 25.54).

19.   The following are all questions formulated by ancient moralists, particularly Stoics. See passages adduced by Ja, CN.

20.   All foods of moderate or low esteem, PNH 16.136, Hor. *S.* 2.2.117, Cic. *Fin.* 2.91. 'pilchards' (*maena*), lit. 'mendole', see D. W. Thompson, *A Glossary of Greek Fishes* (London, 1947) s.v. MAINĤ.

21.   A blunt rejection of philosophy from one of its natural opponents. (Answered with a parable vv.88ff., perhaps having ironical reference to the word 'invalid' (*aegroti*, v.83), of the sick who neglect or refuse treatment. Cf. Cas. on v.88.)

    Solon; Athenian sage, statesman and poet, *fl.* 600 B.C.

    Arcesilas; president and reviver of the Athenian Academy, mid-third century B.C.

    'From nothing nothing . . . etc.' scoffs at a main physical doctrine of the Epicureans and others (see Lucr. 1.150, Merrill ad loc.).

    Fasting ('miss your dinner'): a means to, and a mark of, self-sufficiency more mentioned by outsiders than by philosophers themselves, Aristoph. *Clouds* 416, Hor. *S.* 2.3.257, Plato *Symp.* 220a; cf., however, Epict. *Diss.* 3.13.21.

22.   The third day may be critical, an outing thereon premature: Cels. 3.4.11 and Loeb ed. ad loc., 3.5.2. For the symptoms (below, 95) cf. v.63 and n.18.

    On Sorrentine wine for invalids PNH 14.64; wine as a present to sick clients Juv. *Sat.* 5.32; consumption of snacks (below, v.102) and wine was regular in public baths, Balsdon p. 31 and n. 94, Mayor on Juv. 8.168; *hot* wine (v.101) to promote sweating, Sen. *Ep.* 122.6.

23.   A dinner (*epulis* 98, OLD) eaten, I take it, at the rich friend's house, the meal being the occasion of the preceding snatch of conversation.

24.   The colour, '*white* belly' (cf. also above, v.95; lit. 'your skin's *yellow* . . . ') describes the ill-health of the Mediterranean rather than the North-European complexion.

25.   A Roman funeral: trumpets (Hor. *S.* 1.6.42ff.), lights (for an untimely death, Sen. *Brev. Vit.* 20.5), body embalmed and laid feet towards door (Hom. *Il.* 19.212 and Schol., PNH 7.46, Sen. *Ep.*12.3). Custom and Fitness (Serv. *Aen.*

6.223) bade male next-of-kin carry the bier: sons wore veiled heads (Plut. *Q.R.* 14.267a). Our man has only 'new Romans', manumitted under his will, to carry him, and their head-covering (*capite induto*, v.106) is the *pilleus* (illust. by DS s.v. 481b), the hat that marks them free citizens (Plaut. *Amph.* 462). Cf. Livy 38.55.2 for a freeman's duty at a funeral.

26. For the two methods of taking the pulse see Val. Max. 5.7. Ext. 1, Julian *Misopogon* 348a. Persius is free of the warning symptoms listed by Celsus 2.4.4.

27. According to some this passage is composed of two separate challenges ('Feel your pulse . . . your heart!' and 'Feel your . . . finger-ends!'—for ambiguity because of the absence of personal pronouns cf. Appendix B n.1) from the Friend, or the Doctor-figure of the previous episode, or from the Poet as moral critic, each challenge being answered, 'No fever . . . !' . . . 'No chill . . . !' by someone else—a fresh impersonal Interlocutor or the Sluggard of vv. 1ff., cf. Ja, Nem., Bo, Rudd. Yet it seems a little lame that the Moralist should propose tests to reveal symptoms of (moral) disease when the kind of factor he thinks of as typically causing those symptoms is fairly clearly absent (vv. 109bff., '*If* you catch sight of . . . etc.'), so that the tests' negative results are a foregone conclusion. The transition which the passage affords thus seems weak and is gratuitously long and complex, for its content have partially to be repeated (v. 111a, 'does your heart . . . etc.?'). Also it seems somewhat inconsequential in the ensuing argument that the Moralist, having in vv. 109b-111a combatted the Interlocutor's denial concerning his first test (pulse-rate), does not go on directly and in due order to answer the denial concerning the second test (temperature) that was one of his original pair of challenges. Instead he postpones his answer until vv. 115ff. and allows to intervene a relatively lengthy section on his adversary's mouth-ulcer. This, further, is not apt to be discovered by either of the tests he initially had suggested. ('Let's try your appetite'—lit. 'throat, gullet', v.113a—could be interpreted as the suggesting of an extra test; but then v.113b—lit. 'there's a hidden ulcer in your . . . mouth'—would imply that such an ulcer existed; whereas it seems likely that, conformably with the other symptoms mentioned in this passage, the ulcer is a sign of moral disease and consequently its existence is not to be taken necessarily as a fact, see Ja, Duebner, Bo, cf. Nem., VP.) The interpretations of CN, Cl, Sciv., whose general lines I follow, are without the lameness. They are also without the inconsequence: for the Moralist, though basing his argument for the most part upon the challenges concerned with heart-rate and temperature, is well in order if he refers to other types of symptom, since his only purpose is to answer the implication of his adversary's challenges, namely that the person who issues them is in all respects healthy. Cf. Cas. on v.107, also *Latomus* 32.1973.547

28. On which see J. André, *L'Alimentation et la Cuisine à Rome* (Paris, 1961) pp.18, 31.

29. Commonly an example of insanity, cf. Varro's *Orestes vel de Insania* (Gell.

1. A confrontation between youth, beauty, precocity, wealth, on the one hand and the Sage on the other, fruitful of ethical possibilities; previously exploited in Plato's *Symposium,* the Platonic *Alcibiades* I and II and by other philosophical writers. See Dessen pp. 58-60.
2. 'bearded master, victim . . . etc.', i.e. Socrates, see Plato, *Phaedo, fin.* See also 1.133 and n.42.
    'Ward of Pericles' (perhaps Athens' most powerful statesman), i.e. Alcibiades. Mention is made of this wardship and of A.'s attitude towards it in the Platonic *Alcibiades* I, 104b.
3. *Quirites* is exclusively a title of Roman (not Athenian) citizenry assembled, but P.'s basic concern is not with historical verisimilitude but with morals, cf. vv. 25ff., Appendix C, p.115
4. For this metaphor cf. Epict. *Diss.* 2.11.13, also 1.28.28f. Horace (*Epl.* 2.2.44) had sought to recreate it in literary Latin (drawing upon colloquial sources, cf. Sen. *Apocol.* 8 *fin.,* Plin. *Ep.* 5.9.6) by writing *curvum* ('bent') as opposite of *rectum* ('right'/'straight') in place of *pravum* ('wrong', originally 'crooked'). P. here repeats and elsewhere (3.52, 5.38) extends and varies the idea.
5. Lit. *theta,* the Greek letter Θ, signifying θάνατος, death, and cognate words; familiar as such at Rome. Used in epitaphs, as a judge's and perhaps as a critic's condemnation-mark. Cf. Anc. Comm., Isid. *Orig.* 1.3.8, L-S, LS s.v.
6. Lit. 'pure Anticyras'. There were three towns of this name in Greece; all produced hellebore, herbal remedy for insanity, cf. Sat. 1, n.17.
7. Sunbathing was a favoured pastime, see documentation in Mayor's n. on Juv. *Sat.* 11.203.
8. Alcibiades' mother, a lady of the Alcmeonid Family, gives him good claims to nobility of blood.
9. The name is chosen advisedly (cf. the story of Baucis and Philemon, Ov. *Met.* 8.624-724) to represent humble and aged peasanthood compared with lofty rank.
    Aphrodisiac qualities of the herb basil are mentioned by PNH 20.123.
10. I take vv.23-32 to be a riposte by Alcibiades. He makes and illustrates the statement that criticism is too common and too lightly given. For speech-distribution and interpretation in this satire, see Appendix C.
11. i.e. regard the faults of others, not their own – a metaphor recalling the fable of Phaedrus, 4.10; cf. Cat. 22.21, Hor. *S.* 2.3.299.
12. More lit. 'is too big for a kite' (the bird) 'to fly over', 'big enough to tire a kite' cf. Otto, *Sprichw.* s.v. *milvus* (4).
13. 'chapel', Lat. *compita,* cf. Anc. Comm. 'places like towers at crossroads, where farmers hold sacrifices when their work is at an end . . . etc.' For illust. of these shrines (of the *Lares Compitales,* guardians of the crossroads and its neighbourhood) see cover design (from DS s.v. *compitum*).

The reference is to the Compitalia, a moveable winter festival. For the hanging up of the plough as marking a holiday cf. Tib. 2.1.5f., K. F. Smith ad loc.

The slaves' 'festal treat' is the most basic fare (see Juv. *Sat.* 11.108, ctr. Cato *R.R.* 57 and 58).

For a (?) related portrait of the suitably generous celebration of the Compitalia see Calp. Sic. 4.125f., whose 'Chapel with its through-passage' (*pervia compita*) may lie behind P.'s curious *pertusa* (lit. 'bored-through' 'with hole(s) in'). The upkeep of such shrines probably depended on the generosity of local magnates , cf. DS, PW s.v. *Compitum.*

14. See n.7. With the reading *figas* in v.33 the meaning would be e.g. 'stabbing (fixing) the sun into your skin'.

15. Removal of hair from (male) body and limbs and, much worse, from genitals and anus, indicates pathic dandyism. Documentation from Juvenal, Martial, Clement of Alexandria (who mentions it as a practice carried out in public) in Ja. Means to its achievement, apart from ointments, were tweezers, resin and hot pitch: hence 'spongy' (*marcentis*), 'boil' (cf. *elixas*).

16. Some would favour the tr. e.g. 'worm' (= penis) taking *gurgulio* as a form of *curculio,* 'weevil'. However the Anc. Comm. seems to take the word as I do, and one might quote Pl. *Aul.* 304 *inferiorem gutturem* as a similar metaphorical use of an upper part of the body for a lower one. Cf. also, probably, the image of 6.72.

17. Lit. 'present our legs for arrows', i.e. present a target for sniping ciriticism. The phrase (*praebemus crura*) is probably a sporting term from a ball-game, cf. Isid. *Orig.* 18.69.2. To judge from our passage and Plut. *Cic.* 17.2 it denotes some kind of feint, with attendant risks.

18. A Homeric/Vergilian object, see V.A. 5.312f, Conington ad loc. Persius, however, (cf. Sil. It. 10.181) thinks of *balteus* as the belt, not the sword- or quiver-sling. The Roman military belt was of leather surfaced with decorative metal plates, cf. G. Webster, *The Roman Imperial army,* (London, 1969) p. 127, fig. 13.

19. These words denote dubious practices in the world of business and/or law, but the precise meaning of the phrase *multa vibice flagellas,* 'with many a lash you ply your scourge in (on)' is, now at least, obscure. It perhaps means 'you are the terror of' (CN quoting Hor. *Epl.* 1.15.31) or perhaps, more technically 'drive hard onwards' of the unremitting pursuit of profit, see refs. of Ja, Bud ed. on Mart. 2.30.4. See also the discussion of CN.

'world of affairs', lit. The Puteal ('Well-Head'), for which see Platner-Ash p. 434, F.M. Nichols, *The Roman Forum* (London and Rome, 1877) pp. 127. It was perhaps the stone plinth of a *bidental* (see Sat. 2 n.9) standing at the eastern corner of the Roman Forum, and was a hub of affairs financial, legal or both. Because of the clipped familiarity of authors' references to it, its precise connotations were uncertain even in late antiquity, see Wickham on Hor. *S.* 2.6.34-5.

20. Lit. Cerdo, a personal name, particularly or exclusively of slaves; see examples in CN. Cf. 6.56,60.
21. Possibly imperative: 'See . . . !', 'Recognise . . . !'

1. A frequent theme of Stoic morals cf. Ja p. 181, CN on v.131. On Cornutus (who speaks vv.5-18) see OCD, VE pp. 47-102, PW s.v. *Annaeus* (5).
   There are studies of the language and imagery of the poem in Br (ch. 1, see also index locorum) and by W. S. Anderson, *Ph.Q.* 39. 1960.66-81.
2. For examples of this motif in epic or epicising poetry cf. CN.
3. Again, as once before (cf. Hor. *S.* 2.1.11-15 to which v.4 alludes, and *C.* 1.19.11f.) a contemporary theme for historical *epic*, cf. B. H. Warmington, *Nero* (London, 1969) pp. 87-97. For the ambiguities in P.'s expression see Ja, CN.
4. Ingredients are: names (Procne, Thyestes) recalling myths frequently treated in high poetry, especially tragedy, in which murdered children were cooked for a parent to eat (cf. OCD s.vv.); and Glyco (Sucré, cf. L-S, s.vv. γλύκων, γλυκύς) a first-century actor of whom the Anc. Comm. gives details. (Cf. CN.) For 'pot-boiling' cf. Petron. *Sat.* 38 sub fin., Otto, *Sprichw.* s.v. *olla.*
   Helicon: mountain sacred to the Muses, in Boeotia, cf. Prol. v.4 and n.2.
5. Three caricatures of the 'inspired bard'. The first originated at least as early as Horace (*S.* 1.4.19-20, here imitated). The third (see Anc. Comm.) may refer to the schoolboy's trick of popping the cheeks.
6. *iunctura:* literary technical term used by Horace (*A.P.* 47-8, here imitated; 242) of 'semantic collocation' of words in poetic composition, and by others and by P. himself (cf. Sat. 1 n.21) in related though not always identical senses. See OLD s.v., Brink, KH ad locc. Hor.
7. Where Thyestes (see n.4), having eaten his children's flesh, was presented by his brother Atreus with their *heads,* hands and *feet.*
8. Or 'let my leaves bulge with dismal' (or 'ornate', *bullatis*) 'trivia and lend . . . '
9. Insignia of youth: 'Purple' (30) denotes synecdochically the purple-bordered *toga praetexta,* formal dress for freeborn boys and girls (Isid. *Orig.* 19.24.16, Cic. *Verr.* 2.1.113, 152, PW sub *tirocinium fori* 1451.35ff., Wilson AR pp. 130-1); for 'protection' idea cf. Quint. *Decl.* 340 fin. About 'my pendant' (*bulla,* 31) not all things are clear (cf. passages in Mayor Juv. 5.164, 165, Becker pp. 183-4, Blümner p. 306, Ja ad loc., *Abergl.* p. 44 n. 53, DS s.v. with illust.). A gold pendant, perhaps originally an amulet against the Evil Eye, was worn by sons (and perhaps daughters) of an upper stratum of Society, perhaps *equites* and above. Both items were laid aside, and the pendant, at least, dedicated to the family-gods (Lares, v.31, see OCD² s.v.; 'girdled' — see Frazer, Ov. *F.* 2.634, DS s.v. figg. 4349, 4350) by boys at about sixteen (cf. *Life of P.,* Appx. E, lines 12f; but negotiable, MM pp. 128-131, Balsdon p. 12 and n. 121) in their coming-of-age ceremony (Blümner pp. 335-7) when they received instead the adult's toga. This, and therefore also its Fold, (*umbo,* 33 a fashion-feature of drapery, Tert. *de Pall.* 5 init., Becker p. 415, Blümner p. 2 perhaps distinctively purple on the *t. praetexta* cf. Wilson AR fig. 38a and p. 46) was plain white. On the ensuing freedom and moral dangers, MM

86

p. 127, Apul. *Apol.* 98, Ov. *F.* 3.777-8, and refs of Ja on the present passage. Subura (v.32): busy, central, commercial, prostitute-encumbered area of Rome, see Platner-Ashby s.v., Ja.

10. A long-established metaphor, cf. 3.56 and n.17, Xen. *Mem.* 2.1.20ff.

11. For the metaphors cf. 4.11-12 and n.4; 3.20ff. and n.9.

12. (In explanation of the unity of spirit and activity between P. and Cornutus) a use of astrological ideas which is allusive (to Hor. *C.* 2.17.15-24) and (although systematic Stoicism did generally countenance the very prevalent practices of professional astrology, see PW 2.1813.10ff.) fanciful, cf. CN on v.46. Predominant considerations in predictions are a person's *Day* and *Moment* of birth from which is reckoned (in various ways and in varying detail as dates, types and sophistication of theories vary) the then configuration of the Heavens. One astral *Sign* which is, or contains, the Horoscope proper, and again variously reckoned, is fo particular importance as solely or specially influential at this moment, or at least as the essential basis for further calculation.

For an exposition how friendships may be predicted from congruences between two astrological genitures see Ptolemy, *Tetrabiblos* 4.7 (191-2), with A. Bouché-Leclercq, *L'Astrologie Grecque*, Paris, 1899) pp. 453-4.

The bad and good influences respectively of *Saturn* and *Jupiter* are widely recognised by astrologers and others (Ptol. *Tetr.* 1.5.19, C.C.A.G. V.iii pp. 100f. ap. Housman, *Classical Papers* II, p. 854, CQ 7.1913 p. 21 , Prop. 4.1.83-4). On planets acting to modify each other cf. Ptol. *Tetr.* 2.8.88. But the idea that the 'double' signs, Scales and Twins, are influential for friendly unity of hearts seems to be purely imaginative (Housman, *Classical Papers* II, p. 854 n.1, CQ 7.1913.20 n.1, cf. KH ad loc. cit. Hor. on *Scorpios formidolosus*). Cf. in general Bouché-Leclercq op. cit. pp. 83-6, 383-9, 489-91, 546ff., PW s.v. *Astrologie.*

13. The extra verse (see App. Crit. v.52) recorded in a three-line fragment from the margin of a MS of Venantius Fortunatus means (e.g.) 'their talk, their face, life, inclinations differ universally'. Kugler loc. cit. has interesting nn. on the line's genuineness and the philosophical content of its context.

14. On the eastern pepper-trade see E. H. Warmington *The Commerce between the Roman Empire and India* (Cambr., 1928) pp. 181ff., cf. J. I. Miller, *The Spice Trade of the Roman Empire 29 B.C. - A.D. 641* (Oxford, 1969). Like their Eng. equivalent the words *piper, πέπερι* are familiarly used names for a group of pungent imported spices, although ancient (even scientific) writers, e.g. PNH 12.26ff., are less than fully acquainted with their precise nature, sources and varieties, see PW s.v. *Pfeffer,* E.E. Stanford, *Economic Plants,* (N.Y. 1934) pp. 471-4. They hold, too, (cf. PNH 20.159f., Hor. *Epl.* 1.19.17f.) that eating the seeds of the cummin-plant (also imported, cf. A. C. Johnson, *Econ. Survey of Anc. Rome* II, ed. T. Frank, Baltimore, 1936, p. 3) produces pallor.

15. Lit. 'the Campus (Martius)' see CN, D, Strabo 5.3.8.

16. On *cheragra* (v.58) see W. A. R. Thomson, M.D., *Black's Medical Dictionary* 27th ed. (London, 1967) s.v. *Gout,* W. G. Spencer, Loeb ed. of Celsus, vol. I. pp. 463-5.

17. 331-232 B.C. Succeeded Zeno (the founder) and preceded Chrysippus (cf. 6.8ℓ as head of the Stoic school at Athens. See OCD, A. C. Pearson *The Fragments of Zeno and Cleanthes* (Cambr. 1891) pp. 35ff.

18. More lit. 'Let tomorrow stay the same.' Reading *fiet*, tr. e.g. 'You'll say the same to-morrow'.

19. 'John Citizen', lit. 'Any Publius of the Veline (tribe)', cf. the usage at 6.56, 60, also Hor. *S.* 2.5.32, *Epl.* 1.6.52.

    A rendering 'not the kind that gets any J. C. who qualifies . . .' might be possible (*ut quisquis* for *qua quicumque*, E. Löfstedt, *Vermischte Stud. zur lat. Sprachk. u. Synt.* (Lund, 1936), pp. 9f., G. W. Williams, CR n.s. 8.1958. 209), cf. the more usual phraseology at 1.127. The version in the text follows CN, Housman CQ 7.1913.23f. (*Classical Papers* II, p. 856f.).

20. A Roman personal name, Marcus (vv.79ff., cf. MM p. 26), the citizen's hat ('paraphernalia' v.82, see Sat. 3, n. 25) and the corn-dole-ticket (v.74, cf. May Juv. 7.174) are privileges of the freed slave's citizenship, his *liberty*, as are his rights (vv.79ff.) to engage in civil business in which a slave was severely disabled cf. BRLS pp. 434, 82ff. His master's turning him (vv.75-6, 78; ?to face-about, a 'sign of separation', App. *B.C.* 4.135 with Paul. ex Fest. *manumitti*) and the being touched with a rod (*vindicta* cf. Hor. *S* 2.7.76, Gaius *Inst.* 4.16; see below vv.88, 125, also *festuca*,175) were symbolic items in the most formal type of liberation-ceremony. See H. J. Roby *Roman Private Law* I p. 26 n.1, BRLS pp.441-2, 451ff., and in general Blümner pp. 297f. The point – that (civil) freedom is so little guarantee of moral freedom as to be a misnomer – is made in similar terms, with similar intelligence and with greater clarity by Epictetus *Diss.* 2.1.26-8, q.v. On 'Marcus' (repeated) see J.N. Adams, CQ 28.1978.161f., 164f.

21. (False) syllogising – a Stoic study cf. Pohlenz I pp.50-1; with etymology, cf. ibid. p. 42, SVF II. §§ 156ff. For the major premise cf. Epict. *Diss.* 4.1.1 Brutus: the Tarquin-expeller, 'liberator of the State', Livy 1.60.2.

22. Masurius Sabinus, the jurist, still living in Nero's time and spoken of by Epict. *Diss.* 4.3.12, see S-H II. § 489, H. F. Jolowicz, *Historical Introdn. to Roman Law* (3rd Edn. by B. Nicholas) pp. 378-82. On *rubrica* ('paragraph', v.90) red-written headings of laws, see locc. citt. by Mayor, Juv. 14.192.

23. A widely influential concept, associated especially with Stoicism, e.g. SVF III.79.38-41, index s.v. νόμος, Seneca ap. CN a.h.l. Contrast with human legislation is not infrequent. See De Vogel §§ 1065-76, Pohlenz I pp. 131-4.

    The ignorant man goes wrong in *everything* (say the Stoics: Plut. *de aud. poet.*25c cf. SVF III.124.4-6) with the result here stated, and presently illustrated and (119-123) recapitulated. Cf. SVF III.140.8-10.

24. Of your scales. See Sat. 1, n.4.

25. The sea-god, cf. Verg. *Geo.* 1.437, Ov. *Met.* 4.512ff.

26. For the relationships, in Stoic doctrines of moral decision and action, betwe reason, 'impressions'/'percepts' (*species, visa, φαντασίαι*) and impulse (*impet*

ὁρμή) see Pohlenz I, pp. 88-92, Sen. *Ep.* 113.18.

"The first and greatest task of the philosopher is to *test percepts and discriminate* between them . . . Consider . . . the *assaying of the coinage* . . . " Epict. *Diss.* 1.20.7-9, dramatised and filled out by 2.18.15-29. See also e.g. '(sense-) impression', Loeb ed. index; also Cic. *Acad. Pr.* 2.67.

For the place, in ethical discussion, of other terms and concepts used in this catechism, cf. S. Emp. *Adv. Math.* 11.200-1, Cic. *Acad.* 2.23, J. S. Reid on *artem vivendi*, Epict. *Diss.* 4.1.63; SVF index s.vv αἱρετός, φευκτός; ibid. ἐπιθυμία, Sen. *Const. Sap.* 14.1; ibid. 15.5; Sen. *Vit. B.* 20.5, Epict. (much deeper than either P. or Sen.) *Diss.* 2.22, esp. 34-6; Sat. 6 n.1 and vv.19-26, Sen. *Vit. B.* 20.4; ibid. 20.3, Hor. *Epl.* 1.16.63-4. The Anc. Comm. relates the 'coin fast in the mud' (111-12) to a schoolboy's prank like that of the modern 'abandoned' (but screwed-down) sixpence.

27. i.e. approved . . . disapproved, cf. 4.13, 1.110, 2.1 and n., Hor. *S.* 2.3.246.

'Somewhat later' (*prius . . . mox*): at *Diss.* 2.18.25-6 Epictetus implies that a good 'percept' will induce a successful, action-producing approval more readily than a bad 'percept' will induce a disapproval of the same kind; and that moral strength to feel this kind of disapproval is the product of training and time.

28. Balletic dancer and choreographer, co-originator of Pantomime, fl. Augustus's reign, see PW, Ja, cf. KH on Hor. *Epl.* 2.2.125.

29. Lit. Strigils, one of the toilet-articles regularly carried to the baths by slaves, see Ja. Use and illustrations, Becker's *Gallus*, DS.

30. Whose aperient properties are mentioned Athen.*Deipn.* 1.32e, cf. PNH 14.78, Hor. *S.* 2.4.27ff.; which last (*si . . . morabitur . . . non sine Coo. lubrica . . .*) makes the alternative translation 'shiny Coan (silk)', cf. Prop. 2.1.5, less likely.

31. *verte = muta* 'barter', 'trade'; for *iura* 'swear oaths' (to assure buyers about the quality of goods etc.) cf. Ov. *F.* 5.680-90. This, the interpretation of the Anc. Com., Bo, Duebner, seems bathetic (Ja, VP) and vague; and, in a passage which concentrates closely on the transportation of goods by sea as a means to wealth, is not especially apt to the context.

Alternatives are suggested: (*verte = fac versuram*) 'Borrow money. Swear (you didn't).' Ja. (*verte = averte, verte in/ad te*) 'Steal something. Swear (you didn't).' Cas., D. On oaths in legal procedure see initially Buckland TBORL[3] pp. 529, 633, Justinian *Inst.* 4.6.11, 4.13.4 with nn. of J. B. Moyle, T. C. Sandars. Cf. Dion. Hal. 2.75.3-4, Justinian *Cod.* 4.1.3.

None of these meanings of *vertere* is particularly well-established. It appears to be assimilated to *mutare* at Ov. *M.* 10.157. It is perhaps used for *avertere*, *vertere in se* at Tac. *H.* 1.2. fin., *praemia delatorum invisa (sunt) . . . alii sacerdotia ut SPOLIA adepti, procurationes alii . . . , agerent verterent cuncta* etc.

Ordinances of uncertain date in late legal regulations, the Edict of Theodoric §119 (*Monumenta Germaniae Historica: Legum Tom. V*, ed. H. Brunner, alii, Hanover 1875-89, repr. Stuttgart, 1965, p. 165) and the 'Rhodian Law of the Sea' (on which see H. Kreller *Zeitschr. fur d. gesam. Handelsrecht u.*

Konkursrecht lxxxv. 1921. 257ff., esp. 344-end, and edn. of W. Ashburner, Oxford, 1909) II.14-15, III.13, tell of a process by which, when goods went missing on board ship an oath denying guilt was to be sworn by all on board. Avarice might be commending the vigorous (134-7, 140-2, 146-8) but lucrative (Hor. *C.* 3.6.31-2) life of a ship's master and suggesting the opportunities to interfere with cargo: "Help yourself to some of it. Swear the oath!" This seem apt, and the oath of denial must have been a familiar enough formality for travellers, but there seems no means to show how far back the practice extend before the Edict of T. (c. 500 A.D.); cf. also Petron. *Sat.* 107 sub fin.

32.   More lit. 'You'll have to live content to chisel with a finger at a salt-pot you've licked a second time.' *Terebrare salinum* (for connotations of *salinum*, 'salt-po see 3.25-6 and n.10) is probably proverbial, see CN.

    Succinctus ('shirt-sleeved') just below means 'girt up (for action)' cf. Ja, DS s.v. *cingulum* 1177b and fig. 5615.

33.   A cause of insanity, Sen. *Ep.* 94.17, Hor. *S.* 2.3.141, *Epl.* 2.2.137 which last, together with *Epl.* 2.2.53, probably was in P.'s mind. Cf. Sat. 3 n.5.

    On hemlock see generally PW Suppl. 8, 1956, s.v. *Schierling.* KH on 2.2.53 would suggest that the poets mention hemlock because the patient's conditio is too serious not merely for drugs but even for death to be of much assistanc However there are hints of internal use of hemlock as a medicine at PNH 25. 154, Celsus 5.25.5, Apul. *Apol.* 32, and modern medicine, at least, knows of of it as a sedative in cases including those of 'acute mania' (R. Bentley, H. Tri *Medicinal Plants*, London, 1880, Vol. II, no. 118).

34.   An inferior vintage, cf. Hor. *S.* 2.3.143. The taste may be due to tainting fror the smell of ship's tackle (cf. PNH 14.133; 16.52); but for pitch as a wine-preservative and hints of what the worst wines might taste like see Colum. *De Re Rust.* 12.19.2-3, 20.3, 20.6, 23.2-3.

35.   Reading *'pergant . . . sudare',* tr. (e.g.) 'should go and sweat a g. e.?'

36.   More lit. 'Your living (life) belongs . . . ' A number of (perhaps unnecessary) precise interpretations can be offered, e.g.: 'It's My gift that you live life to t full' (D, ?Ja); 'Your life belongs, is dedicated, to Me' (Anc. Comm., VP); 'In my power is the (kind of) life you have'; 'The life you live is ours (yours-and mine and not Avarice's)' cf. CN; 'All we have is the life you're leading' (cf. C 'None can take from us a life which you've lived to the full' (cf. Sciv., ?Ja); 'Ours to enjoy is the life you lead'; 'Your (very) existence is something gaine (cf. Pretor).

37.   An example taken, as is Epict. 4.1.20 (q.cf., along with Cic. *Parad.* 36, *T.D.* 4.76, precc.) from literature. Terence's *The Eunuch* (adapted from the Gree now lost, of Menander) opens with a scene (well-known, cf. Cic. *N.D.* 3.72, Quint. *Inst.,* e.g. 9.2.11) in which slave and young lover converse in terms li these about the latter's relations with his mistress. Hor. also had used the scene, *S.* 2.3.259-71. P.'s lines allude verbally to both Ter. and Hor., but the is much in the words and something in the sense which comes from neither. Characters' names (and how much besides there is no means to know) come

from Menander, cf. Anc. Comm.

The doors may be wet and the torch gone out *either* because it is raining, cf. Hor. *C*.3.10.19f., A.P. 5.189.2 (VP, D) *or* because scent, wine or tears have been poured on the door (refs., Ja, CN) and because it is late and the torch is spent (cf. Prop. 1.3.10). For the conventions, literary and otherwise, of the ancient love-song at the beloved's door see in general F. O. Copley, *Exclusus Amator* (Monog. of American Philol. Assn. no. XVII, 1956).

38. A thank-offering for deliverance, cf. Cas., edd. on Plato *Phaedo* 118. On the Def. Deities (*dis depellentibus*), TLL s.vv. *depulsor, depulsorius, depellere* (566.59-61), *avertere* 1322.80ff., CIL 13. 5197 comm., cf. L. Gernet *Platon, Lois: Livre IX.* Thèse . . . Univ. de Paris, 1917, p. 70 n. 10 on Plato *Laws* 854b.

39. A different punctuation, commas at the ends of vv.169, 171, produces the following more elaborate expressions, which may be adopted singly or together: (a) " . . . disciplined with her scarlet slipper to teach you not to fuss and gnaw . . . " (*ne* introduces a final clause); (b) " . . . if she called, you'd soon say, 'What shall I do, then . . . ?' " (*haut mora* parenthetic adv. phr. = 'soon'; Davus speaks all from "That's useless!" to " . . . not even now").

40. Perhaps playing purely an acolyte's role in a manumission (see n. 20) at this date (cf. BRLS pp. 442, 452), although evidence (*Dig.* 40.2.8, 40.2.23) concerning the nature and development of the lictor's part in the ceremony is bare and equivocal. For a lictor's functions generally, see OCD.

41. More lit. 'blanced': "The white (*candida*) or whited (*cretata*) toga was the dress of candidates . . . seeking public office . . . It was treated with *creta*" (generic term for industrial clays; suggested identification of the one concerned, R. H. S. Robertson on PNH 35.196ff., CR 63.1949.52) "for extra whiteness and distinction." Isid. *Orig.* 19.24.6.

Munificent provision of public treats by magistrates and would-be magistrates was part of the political mechanism of the municipalities, to which P. is perhaps referring here as at 1.129f., 3.29 (with n.11), 6.48-51, and of Rome (Friedländer, RLM II.pp.10-11, CIL 4.1186, 1190 with pp. 70-1, cf. ILS 6087 Ch. 132, Tac. *Ann.* 4.62.2, M. L. Gordon, JRS 21.1931.73-5). The Floralia ('Fiesta'), on which see PW, was perhaps special in some way as an occasion for such provision (CIL 8.6958, 9.3947, 11.6357, cf. Dio 78/9.22.1). Anc. Comm. would suggest that at it chick-peas (*cicer*) were scattered (with other gifts — for 'General Scramble' as part of public festivities cf. Stat. *Silv.* 1.6.9ff., Mart. 8.78.7ff., CIL 4.1177, 9.1655) as a symbolic Spring tradition.

Distribution of speeches:

The words of encouragement: 'Come on . . . Fiesta' may be spoken (*A*) by Ambition (cf. Avarice, Luxury above) or (*B*) by Persius, ironically.

'And why not?' (*quid pulchrius?*) may be (*a*) a continuing part of the (i) serious or (ii) ironical encouragement, (*b*) an ironical concession by Persius replying to Ambition (cf. *A* above), (*c*) a defence by the man whom the passage as a whole criticises as the slave of Ambition (the defence may be (i) spoken directly by the man or (ii) quoted by the Satirist), (*d*) words of another impersonal interlocutor, (*e*) words of the 'sunny old men'.

I have taken *A* with *c* (ii). *B* with *a* (ii), Ja, CN, Cl. *A* with *b*, VP, D, Sciv., Bo. In general see VP.

42. "The chief piety towards the gods is to have right opinions about them . . . to obey them . . . But it is always appropriate to make libations and sacrifices . . . *after the manner of our Fathers* and . . . not in a slovenly fashion . . . " Epict. *Ench.* 31, cf. Sat. 2.71-5. A different emphasis, Sen. *Ep.* 95.47-50 "(Concerning) worship of the gods . . . Let us not allow the lighting of *lamps* on *Sabbaths.* Gods do not need light and even humans don't like *soot . . .* (Nor) sitting at temple-doors . . . (nor) holding the mirror for Juno . . . Be good. Imitation of the gods is worship enough."

Herod, a name well-known in Horace's day (*Epl.* 2.2.184) and still in P.'s (cf. Dio 60.8.3). For considerable knowledge of (and for attitudes to) Jewish customs among Romans see Tac. *H.* 5.2-5, Mayor on Juv. 14.96-106, cf. *Dict. d'Archéol. Chrét. et de Liturg.* (Paris, 1924-53) s.v. *Judaisme* col. 110. The tunny-fish (*Encycl. Judaica,* Jerusalem, 1971-2, 6.1327, Mishnah, *Shabb.* 22.2, Bab. Talmud, *Shabb.* 35b, 118b) is probably, and the interior lights (B. Talm. *Shabb.* 20b, 35b, Mishn. *Shabb.* 2.4-5, 3.6, Jos. *c. Apionem* 2.282, Budé ed. ad loc.) and wine-and-(brimming?) jar (E. R. Goodenough, *Jewish Symbols in the Greco-Roman Period,* N.Y., 1956, vol. 6 pp. 134-141) are perhaps a further example of such knowledge. Flowers and silent prayer, however, do not seem to belong especially to Jewish ritual either in fact or elsewhere in the ancient imagination (cf. *Encycl. Judaica* s.v. *Flowers: Ceremonial Use,* Juv. 12.90; Sat. 2.8ff., Lucan 5.104f., Juv. 10.289f. and Mayor ad loc., 1 Samuel 1.13).

For red 'Arretine' ware cf. MM pp.659-61. If the 'white jar' is for drinking it could be of glass, PNH 36.198-9.

43. 'Priests performing rites to foresee dangers used to observe an egg placed on a fire to see whether it leaked . . . at the top or at the side. If it burst . . . it portended danger . . . ' — so the Anc. Comm. See PW s.v. *ooskopia.* Eggs in another kind of rite, J. E. Harrison, *Prolegg. to the Stud. of Greek Relig.*[3] (Cambr., 1922) pp. 628f. For scrupulous superstitions cf. Clem. Alex. *Strom.* 7.4.

'Corybants': lit. *Galli,* eunuch-priests of the goddess Cybele, cf. Ov. *F.* 4.179-372, J. G. Frazer on vv.183, 209, 221, 361.

On the rattle of Isis; her worship at Rome; her power to blind (cf. interps of Ja, Sciv.), see Juv. 13.93, Mayor ad loc., Apul. *Met.* 11.4, DS s.v. *sistrum.*

On medicine and magic, prophylactic doses etc., times of day, odd numbe E. Tavenner, *Studd. in Magic fr. Latin Lit.* (N.Y., 1916) pp. 74-5, 105-112, 118-20, cf. Plut. *De superstit.* 168 B-E, Tib. 1.5.9-16. Garlic in (folk-) medici PNH 19.111, Ser. Samm. *Lib. Med.* 29, 184, 330ff., 899, 1027, 1037.

44. More literally, 'centurions . . . for a hundred (*centum*) Greeks . . . a hundred pence (*centusse*) . . . '

1. A subject prominent in Horace's moral writings too, e.g. *S.* 1.29-40, 68-78, 92-107, *Epl.* 1.4.7, 1.7.57, 2.2.190-2, which last is a text developed in vv.22, 33ff. Cf. also *Teletis Reliquiae*, ed. O. Hense (Tübingen, 1909), pp.33.3ff., 37.5ff., with nn., and Sat. 3.69-71.
   On the letter-form in Satire see G. L. Hendrickson, AJP 18.1897.313-24, G. C. Fiske, *Lucilius and Horace* (Madison, 1920), pp. 176-8, 426-7.

2. Friend of P. 'from earliest adolescence', and his posthumous editor (*Life of P.* Appx. E, lines 16-17, 44-5); a lyric poet praised faintly by Quintilian (*Inst.* 10.1.96; fragments, Morel FPL pp. 126-7) and probably a writer on Metric. See B p. 18.

3. Various interpretations are possible, see B pp.21f. (with E. Kenney CR 20.1970. 410, but also Nisbet p. 66 and CQ 29.1979.147 n.1), 23f.

4. Whether Romans' references to poets as musicians are literary convention or to be taken literally is disputed, cf. J. B. Leishman, *Translating Horace* (Oxford, 1956) p. 38 and nn.1, 2.

5. So, I think, Ja pp. 61, 214. The various lyric tones and subjects mentioned have parallels in Horace. Reading *senex* in v.6 (B, Bo, Cl, D, CN) tr. e.g. 'skilled besides, though old, to recount youth's frolics and to write in light, decorous strain'. Discussion of vv.5-6, B pp.26-31.

6. ' . . . Ennius . . . at the beginning of his Annals . . . says that in a dream he saw *Homer,* who told him that he' (Homer) 'had once been a *peacock* and that from the peacock his soul had passed into Ennius, according to the teaching of *Pythagoras*' (i.e. by metempsychosis), Anc. Comm. That passage of Q. (Quintus) Ennius– a claim to Homeric inspiration—was well-known in antiquity: a discussion in Kambylis pp. 191-201, esp. 200. According to B (cf. Housman, CR 48.1934.50f., *Classical Papers* III.1232f.) the line of Ennius which P. quotes, v.9, is from his Satire and not from his *Annals* as Vahlen (V^3, *Ann.* v.16) has it.

7. For these marks of niggardly economy cf. vv.19f., 4.32, Hor. *S.* 2.2.58-62, 2.3.124-6, 143f., PNH 33.26; ctr. vv.68f., Hor. *A.P.* 422, *Epl.* 2.2.133f.

8. Cf. Sat. 5 n.12. Differences between twins were of interest generally (Hor. *S.* 2.1.26-7; cf. *Epl.* 2.2.183-9) and as a problem in astrology, cf. Cas. a.h.l., Augustine *C.D.* 5.2.

9. Cf. vv.68f. and Apicius's recipes *DRC* Bk.3 , also Hor. *S.* 2.2.61-2, 2.3.125. 'by the cup', i.e. as a small quantity for the occasion.
   Pepper was widely-used but not inexpensive, PNH 12.29, PW *Pfeffer,* 1424.

10. Notes on some matters of significance concerning the distribution of lines between speakers and the whole course of argument from this point onward are bulky and interconnected, so they have been placed in an appendix.

11. On ships' gods and other statuary or emblems, Ov. *Tr.* 1.10.1f, Hor. *C.* 1.14.10, G. Luck, KH ad locc. Cf. PW Suppl. 5.934, C. Torr *Ancient Ships*

(Cambridge, 1895) pp. 65-7, nn. and figg., B p. 57 and n.2.

12. See Sat. 1, n. 27.

13. For Romans' anxiety about their treatment at and after burial cf. Blümner pp. 488, 490-1, J. C. M. Toynbee, *Death and Burial in the Rn. World* (London, 1971), pp. 62-3. Funeral Meals: Blümner p. 509, Toynbee pp. 50-1, Ja, Petron. *Sat.* 65 fin.-6. Perfumes: Blümner, p. 501, CN, Juv. 4.109. Casia and cinnamon (not used as food-flavouring before C.9th) would, in view of their appearance, be liable to adulteration with *cherry-bark.* See PW s.v. *Casia* 1637.30ff., 1638.33ff., 1649.1-3, *Encycl. Brit.*[15], *Micropaedia* II p. 614.

14. More lit. 'Are you to reduce the property without suffering for it (*incolumis*; for which alternative renderings are: 'when you've (personally) suffered no (financial) loss', or 'when (unlike your friend) you're safe')?' See further Bo, B pp.63-4, 64 n.6.

15. Lit. Bestius, seemingly well-known as representative 'puritan' critic, cf. Hor. *Epl.* 1.15.37, Wickham ad loc. There are perhaps resemblances between his views on the nutrition of farmhands and the views implicitly attributed to Vettidius at 4.31, where cf. n.13. Cf. also Appx. D.

16. *maris expers,* a vexed phrase, see D and the full discussion of B, pp. 69-77. It occurs in Horace, *S.* 2.8.15, where it probably means 'without seawater' (*maris* from *mare,* 'sea') and this sense, in various constructions and with various meanings ('indigenous, that has not crossed the sea', 'indigestible', 'stupid', 'concentrated', (with irony) 'so-refined'), is often given to it here. According to the version in the text, Horace's original has been still further altered, to 'without masculinity' (*maris* from *mas,* 'male'). The use of *mas* (neuter) in this sense is unparalleled (cf. B p.75 n.28) but neuter adjj. are fairly frequently used as nouns by P., e.g. 2.61, 69, 74, 5.48, 151 and the usage does not appear too difficult. Certainly it gives good sense.

17. Lit. '(from) Caesonia' most durable of the wives of the emperor Caligula (see Suet. *Cal.* 25.3, Dio 59.23.7). For Cal.'s farcical N.-European campaign, 39-40 A.D., and plans for triumph-celebrations cf. Suet. *Cal.* 43-9, Dio 59. 21-3, 25.1-5; also, however, J.P.V.D. Balsdon, *The Emperor Gaius (Caligula)* (Oxford, 1934) pp. 58-95, 220-1, PW 10.418.62-419.43 and foll.

Arms (spoils, for display on temples and the house of the victorious general; cf. Val. Max. 7.6.1, PNH 35.7) and décor for the Parade ('lofty monuments', lit. 'mighty Rhines', figures symbolic of territories conquered, cf. Ja, Bo, Ovid *A.A.* 1.219ff.) are requisites of a Triumph and, on this occasion, mean contracts for manufacturers. Most edd. think that the 'yellow plush' is, or is for, wigs for supposed germanic prisoners (Suet. 47); others, that it refers to garments (cf. TLL *gausape* 1721.12-17). See B.

18. Of gladiators, cf. ILS 6296, 399, 5146, Petron. 45; probably an 'astronomical' number, cf. Hor. *S.* 2.3.85-6, 87, ILS III, p. 731. General information in DS s.v. *Gladiator,* esp. p. 1567b.

19. For the practice and the items mentioned see Ja, CN; cf. Sat. 5 n. 38.

20. The meaning of almost every word of *non adeo . . . iuxta est* (vv. 51-2) is disputed. The only thing fairly certain is that in view of what follows it must be, or must include, a refusal or threatened refusal by the Heir, faced with the Satirist's challenge, to continue as his heir — a considerable misfortune for the Satirist, see B p. 94.

I interpret *exossatus* (lit. 'boned', 'filleted') e.g. 'pulped', 'smashed' (cf. Pl. *Pseud.* 382, *Amph.* 318 and subsequent word-play), a sense in which it should be usable in a metaphorical phrase with *ager* (meaning 'estate'; *(perdere) agrum paternum* Schol. Juv. 6.57) which would match other phrases, such as *devorare patrimonium, rem patris oblimare* (Hor. *S.* 1.2.62). B pp.96f. makes it at least possible that *iuxta est* means 'is available'.

The main difficulties concern (i) *exossatus,* often rendered 'cleared of its *stones*' (a rendering based on a hint in the Anc. Comm. cf. Coffey, p. 241, n. 98) and so 'productive', 'fertile'; or else e.g. 'backboneless' i.e. 'exhausted', and (ii) *adeo,* a verb or an adverb? *non adeo* (sc. *hereditatem*), 'I don't take the inheritance'; or (e.g.) *non adeo . . . exossatus* 'not sufficiently boned, fertile' etc. *iuxta* is usually rendered (e.g.) 'hereabouts'.

Other suggested renderings (for more exhaustive lists, Bo; with attributions, VP; with attributions and discussion, B):

1) The Heir says he refuses to inherit. The Satirist replies that he (still) has a *fertile* estate or a *graveyard cleared of bones* (and so *productive*) hereabouts; or that (even supposing that) he has an *exhausted* estate . . . ; (for this he can easily find an heir).

2) The Heir says he refuses to inherit, and then, either that he has a *fertile* estate of his own; or, that the land hereabouts has been *cleared of stones* (which are lying in piles and may be thrown at him by the crowd (cf. v.42) if they hear him object to the promised largesse in order to save his inheritance); or, that the Satirist's estate here is *exhausted* (with expenditure, and therefore, no longer worth having).

3) The Heir says either that (he will not object because) the land hereabouts is *not sufficiently cleared of stones* (which may be thrown at him . . . etc.); or that the estate here *isn't sufficiently fertile* (either, to support the expenditure; or, to be desirable); however, in this third group of suggestions, only the very last gives something like a clear threat to refuse the inheritance.

21. Lit. 'Virbius's' (name of Hippolytus after resurrection, see B). Prob. because it was a slow climb for passenger-vehicles the hill was a popular pitch for *beggars.* Further details on both points in Anc. Comm., CN.

22. Lit. 'Mercury', cf. 2.44 and n.12, DS s.v. *Mercurius* 1818b-1819, figg. 4853, 4958-61.

23. Reading *vin* one should probably render 'Do you want to appreciate . . . ?'

24. According to some the Satirist continues to speak.

25. Cf. n.9, also P. White, CP 67.1972.61 col. (b).

26. To advertise fine physical condition, cf. Cas., Sen. *Ep.* 80.9.

27. Lit. '(it's coming) . . . into a wrinkle', 'into wrinkles', a pun on the notion 'three (etc.)-*fold*'. Alternatively one could tr. 'into my lapel', 'cuff', 'lap'. See B.

28. Cic. *Acad Pr.* 2.91-2 tr. J. S. Reid: (A Sceptic speaks: reason and dialectic cannot lead to certainty:) 'The nature of the universe has permitted us no knowledge of limits such as would enable us to determine in any case *how far to go*. Nor is it so with the *heap of corn* alone . . . there is no matter whatever concerning which, if questions with gradual increase are put to us (e.g. whether a man is rich or poor . . . whether a number of things are many or few, long or short, broad or narrow), we know how much addition or diminution to make before we can give a definite answer'. Cf. ibid., 49 'they prove that a *heap* results from the addition of a single grain', and nn. of J. S. Reid ad locc.

Chrysippus (c. 280-207 B.C., succeeded third to headship of the Stoic school) tried, without convincing everyone, to circumvent the celebrated (Cic. *Div.* 2.11, Pease ad loc.) philosophical impasse, arising from the indeterminable quality of relative terms, that was exploited to support the Sceptics' position, cf. *Acad. Pr.* 2.93-4, J. M. Rist, *Stoic Philosophy* (Cambridge, 1969) p. 146.

Some attribute the ironical last line to the preceding speaker, determined to continue his activities indefinitely.

'(Persius) left (his) book unfinished. Some lines were removed from the end of the book to give it the appearance of completeness: Cornutus slightly abbreviated it . . . ' *Life of P.* (Appx. E) lines 42ff. It is possible, therefore, that in smaller or greater degree this satire, and especially its ending, is shaped to the editors' need rather than the author's ultimate intention. See B pp. 125-8.

Appendix A, Satire 1

(i)   On the parodies or quotations, vv.71b-5, 78, 93-5, 99-102.

Works mentioned by Korzeniewski p. 418 n. 90 discuss whether P.'s 'citations' are quoted direct from the works of others or are parodies by himself. In particular there are ancient stories, and modern disagreement, about the existence of references in vv.93-5, 99-102 to the poetry of P.'s emperor, Nero. Notes in the Anc. Comm. attribute to Nero the words cited there, but other notes contradict them, (on references to Nero in these nn. see Ja p. LXXIV), and the story perhaps appended late to P.'s *Life* concerning an insult to Nero in v.121 (see app. crit.) must be false (CN, E. J. Kenney, CR (n.s.) 15.1965.120). Cassius Dio 61.20.2 (Cent. 2-3 A.D.) says scornfully that Nero 'performed to the lyre some *Attis* or *Bacchantes'* (cf. vv.93, 99-102, 105), but this is professedly vague in its scorn and it could be an echo of Persius and the stories in his commentators rather than reliable evidence of titles or subjects of poems by Nero. Tac. *Ann.* 14.15-16 and Suet. *Nero* 12, 23-4, 52 are completely unspecific. To authors mentioned by Korzeniewski add VE pp. 218-25, Nisbet p. 47, Rudd pp. 16f.

The greater part of poetry written in P.'s day has not survived, and it is impossible to be certain whether P. was quoting or was parodying and, if parodying, how close the parody is to original texts (see, however, Diomedes GLK 1.499.21ff. below; also the comment in Korzeniewski's note 90, page 418). The same cause makes it additionally difficult to estimate what points in the lines he cites P. considered disagreeably typical of poetry which he disliked. Various estimates are given and, in what follows, I have tried to set down some account of them. P's general descriptions of the type of poetry to which he objects (see Appx. *A.ii*, p. 105; with *molli* 'soft' ('light', 63), *tenerum* ('aesthetic', 98) cf. Prop. 1.7.19, Rothstein ad loc., W. Steidle, *Stud. zu* Ars Poetica *des Horaz*, Würzburg, 1939, pp. 123-4) suggest that it was written by poets whose ideals were derived from those of Callimachus and previous Roman disciples of his (cf. Prol. n.1), general terms for whom are 'neoterics', 'new poets (*novi poetae*)', 'Alexandrian(ism)'. Names of poets in this tradition of Latin poetry and discussion of its development are given briefly by Br pp.180-3. See also references to 'Alexandrians' in L. P. Wilkinson, *Ovid Recalled* (Cambr., 1955), Index of Names. Several clear points of contact with poetry of this tradition emerge from study of P.'s citations, see below.

Parody is present elsewhere in Persius and in the literature of his day, cf. J.P. Sullivan, *The* Satyricon *of Petronius* (London, 1968) pp. 91-2 and ch.V, Korzeniewski p. 421 and OCD[2] on *Einsiedeln Eclogues,* Coffey ch.9 on Seneca's *Apocolocyntosis.*

In translating these citations it seemed desirable to mark them somehow as distinct in style from their context, but it was hopeless to try to reproduce any great number of the points of style picked out below, and I tried other means. The 'poetic' archaism and contortion of word-order to which I resorted occasionally do not reflect similar features in the Latin of the citations when it is compared with

97

the Latin of its surrounding context, and the attempt at verse for vv.99-102 obviously does not imply that these lines are distinct, in *that* way, from their context.

Vv. 71b-5. These lines would not justify the space they take if they were a mere catalogue, for information's sake, of what the persons under discussion cannot do or are not good at doing (cf. Appx. *A.ii,* p.101f. They must be mocking comment b parody (see Br p. 120) and the style supports this conclusion. The use of a great number of items of 'pastoral furniture' without much relief, beginning with a swift list (vv.71b-3a) and accompanied by other potentially homely or mundane images, 'feverishly', 'dressed' (*trepida, induit*), caricatures by exaggeration the pastoral simplicity of the type of passage mentioned in n.22. Even Vergil's list of farm-tools (*G.* 1.160-75) is far more measured and relieved. Ctr. also, from n.22, *V.E.* 7.49f., *G.* 3.375-80, Prop. 4.4.75-80, Tib. 1.1.6ff., 2.5.87ff., Ov. *Am.* 3.13.13ff. Lacking a more dignified context, the juxtaposition of the words 'oxen' and 'Dictator' (v.74, *boves dictatorem*) only looks incongruous (Br p. 120 n.3) and the elaborate alliteration of v.72, f-, p-, f-, P-, f- and the assonance *terens dent-* (73) are only pretty. The synecdoche 'share-head/plough-sole' for 'ploughshare' (the part of the plough most obviously rubbed in the furrow, *V.G.* 1.46) might also have seemed rather precious or even (considering the abundance of agricultural terms) technicall inaccurate, once the reader became aware of the parody. The relatively intricate syntax (*ubi corbes . . . , terens . . . cum . . . , unde . . .*) could also be some kind of comment on contemporary poetry. Cincinnatus, a main figure in a passage, whethe of 'Heroic Thoughts' or of pastoral simplicity, is not mentioned except by apostrophes (cf. E. Norden, *P. Vergilius Maro, Aeneis Buch VI,*[4] Stuttgart, 1957, pp. 122, 126).

If it is correct to say that the passage leads into and includes an example of 'Utterance of Heroic Thoughts' (see n.22 and Ap ɔx.A.ii pp.100-2), the great quant 'pastoral furniture' in and around the account of Cincinnatus would emphasise the failure or refusal of modern fashions of poetry to give dignity to such subjects. Thi impression would be increased by the use of the word *uxor* for 'wife' (74). With hardly an exception, true epic poetry prefers *coniunx,* e.g. 'spouse'. The parody would then mock poets who could express ideas of heroism only in unreal, romant or otherwise inappropriate terms. It is conceivable that the surviving line attributed to Attius Labeo (vv.4, 50, Ja p. 248) contains elements (*manduces, pisinnos*) that would expose it to this kind of attack.

V. 78. Appropriately, a contrast with vv.71b-5. *Aerumnis,* 'woe' is a lofty poe word (TLL s.v. *aerumna* 1066.47-50), used in parody by Lucilius, ROL III p. 235 v.729. *Luctificabile,* 'lamentatious' (not elsewhere found?) is a would-be lofty, larg bodied word of a type favoured by the old tragedians, cf. Ja, ROL II p. 165 v.12 and n.(*b*), and parodied by Lucilius, ROL III p. 235 v.726, cf. Müller DRM p. 86.

The syntax too is poetic, cf. (for *cor* 'accusative of reference' with *fulta*) LH pp. 36-7, E. C. Woodcock, *A New Latin Syntax* (London, 1959) §19.

Vv. 93-5, 99-102. The following estimates of what P. found offensive in the fragments he quotes or creates as parody are drawn in considerable part from the comments and references of CN, Rudd pp. 174f. and Br pp. 127, nn.1, 2, 129, n.1, which too may be consulted. Cf. also VE pp. 198-201, 208-18, Müller DRM pp. 154f.

As has been said (nn.28, 32), the cults of Cybele, v.93, cf. v.105, and Bacchus, vv.99-102, cf. 105, are strongly represented in the content of the passages criticised by P. It seems possible that he found cause for complaint in a regularly-to-be-anticipated treatment of exotic frenzy, especially in delicately-phrased verse (see below). The story of Attis's self-emasculation no doubt was a contributory reason for P.'s (and Martial's, n. 28) selection of him to typify a fashionable effeminate style of verse.

Various stylistic features of the lines can be noted. Many of them are seen also in extant works of 'neoteric' poets (cf. above, also Prol. with nn.1, 2, 4), whose successors and imitators P. seems to be opposing. Some items of phraseology are reminiscent of this poetry (D, Br nn. citt.) as is the part played by the echo (102, cf. Br p. 129, n.1, also (?) Mart. 2.86.3). The sounds (*o, r, m, b*) of v.99 probably imitate the sound-painting of Cat. 64.261ff. or something similar. The exotic imagery (see nn.28, 32) includes the use of seven names and five other words of Greek morphology (listed, Br p. 129 n.1, cf. Kroll on Cat. 64.15,35 and *Stud.* pp.21f., V. *Aen.* 4.301-3, Caesius Bassus fr. 2M). In vv.93, 94 the line is completed by a group of two such words, cf. refs. of Bo on v.93 and general similarities with refs. of Kroll, *Stud.* p. 21, also the comment of Rudd on v.93. There is the metrical 'point' of having a spondee in place of the usual dactyl in the fifth foot of an hexameter, *Āppēn(nino)* v.95, Kroll *Stud.* p. 21, Fordyce on Cat. 64.3, although he seems wrong about the post-Vergilian use of this feature. A noun regularly has a 'poetic' decorative epithet, but the two stand apart, being artistically arranged. Often one immediately precedes the central caesura and the other concludes the line, and there is a rhyming effect between their endings (*longo . . . Appennino* v.95, cf. 99, 100). V.99 is so arranged that in addition each of two epithets is transferred and agrees grammatically with the noun to which logically the other belongs, 'double enallage' (Kroll *Stud.* p. 277 and on Cat. 64.50, VE p. 212, L. P. Wilkinson, *Ovid Recalled,* Cambr., 1955, p. 40, LHS p. 160). Alliteration is absent, cf. LHS p. 701; elision also is absent and v. 102 may exemplify an excessive tendency to dactylic movement, cf. Appx. A(ii) p.107, VE pp. 200, 211, C. H. Keene, ed. *The Eclogues of Calpurnius Siculus,* London, 1887, p. 15, M. Platnauer, *Lat. Elegiac Verse,* Cambridge, 1951, pp. 72, 36f., L. P. Wilkinson op. cit. p. 150, and *Golden Latin Artistry,* Cambridge 1963, p. 131f.,

In view of P.'s general criticism of the refinement, modernity, smoothness or effeminacy of the poetry which is his butt, the following points may also be of interest as contributing to an overall effect of that type:

According to Quintilian, *Inst.* 9.4.65, the covering of two metrical feet by one word at the end of an expression is 'even in verse, unduly effeminate' (i.e. smooth and formless(?); 'gliding with ongoing speed of pronunciation' (?) Diomedes, GLK 1.469.20, L. P. Wilkinson, CQ 34.1940.37 and n.2), and among other instances he quotes the hexameter-ending *Appennino* (v.95; extant examples in Br p. 127 n.2).

99

Diomedes GLK 1.499.21ff. praises a line very like v.99 as 'nicely rounded . . . with (?) rapid fluency and well-managed connexions of words'. Cf. v.92 and n. 21. In addition to the absence of elision, the other precepts for smooth 'jointure' (*iunctura* cf. v.92 and n.21) given by Quintilian, *Inst.* 9.4.33-42 (cf. Cic. *de Or.* 3.172), sufficiently unexacting it is true, are observed. Greek 'y'-sounds (vv.93, 101) are spoken of as 'sweet' by Quint. *Inst.* 12.10.27 (cf. v.34 and n. 13). The future participle (vv.100-1, *ablatura, flexura* 'fain to . . .') seems not to have been used in this way by poets before Vergil, LHS p. 390, cf. also CN on v. 100. The (?) metaphor *costam* ('rib', v.95) and the metonymy *Nerea* ('Neptune', v.94) seem rather extravagant, CN ad locc., Rudd p. 174; cf., perhaps, the fragment '*alveum lintribus arent* . . . ' etc., Sen. *Ep.* 114.5. *reparabilis* ('repairing, reviving, revival-', v.102) seems always to be passive elsewhere, 'reparable', LS, cf. Ja.

The way into plain grotesqueness is opened on at least three occasions: the phrases 'dividing blue Neptune' and 'proud calf('s head)', which is ineptly created from the Greek of Euripides, *Bacch.* 743; and the identical position in the line of the two future participles in vv.100-1.

(ii)   On vv.63-82

It is possible to interpret these lines ('What says the public – cavort on the benches?') in a large number of ways, with various punctuations and distributions of speeches. There are two areas of major difficulty, vv.69-75, 76-8:

69-75
(a) The opening words of the sentence 69-75 would most naturally herald criticism of present-day "utterance of Heroic Thoughts"; for it seems to draw a contrast between the *aim* of uttering 'Heroic Thoughts' (heroas *sensus*) and the powers of those accustomed to toying with Greek (nugari *solitos Graece*), who are committed to (but for reasons of lack of experience are obviously unfitted for) the task of uttering them.

(b) Because of its characteristics (cf. Appx. *A.i*) it is plausible to say that the example — 'baskets, hearth etc. . . Remus. . . . etc.'— is a mocking parody of present day writing.

(c) The interpretation usually given to this passage is that it is spoken by P. a shows the ridiculousness of teaching utterance of Heroic Thoughts in the circumstances here envisaged and currently fashionable. The inexperienced writers who aspire to deliver such material cannot produce even poetic commonplaces (school-exercises). How much less, then, could they produce Heroic Thoughts? However, on this supposition

(i) It must count as curious that, whereas the passage begins (see (a)) as if me ing to criticise present-day utterance of Heroic Thoughts, all (according to m edd. CN, Sciv., Bo(?), Br) the parody seems to be aimed at poetic common-places (or school-exercises, see n.22) concerning "Praises of Rich Countrysic Therefore the parody which forms the main part of the passage does not dea with what apparently was to have been its main subject.

(ii) It must also count as curious that the writing criticised in the parody (see (b)) is apparently noticed as something which those who 'toy with Greek' and are taught 'utterance of Heroic Thoughts' *cannot* do (cf. *neque . . . didicerint* Anc. Comm., paraphrases of VP, D). Therefore the parody which forms the main part of the passage does not deal, either, with the activities of those who seemed likely to be the main target of criticism.

(iii) It must count as curious, thirdly, that what is mainly parodied (vv.71b-5) and thus rejected, would nevertheless, on the face of it, have improved the performance of the poets attempting Heroic Thoughts, had they cultivated it (70-1). Therefore that which we should expect to be represented as a good thing, even if to only a very limited extent, is ridiculed fairly elaborately and at some length.

(d) The parody of "Praises of Rich Countryside" seems to incorporate material (Remus and Quintius, vv.73-5) which might be classed as 'Heroic Thoughts', especially by an audience which has just heard mention of this phrase at v.69.

The version in the text (cf. n.22) assumes, in answer to (c.i, iii) that what vv.71b-5 parody is not merely the way in which poetic commonplaces (or school-exercises) of countryside-description are in general written, but the way in which modern writers with some rudimentary ability at these descriptions might be supposed to approach the "utterance of Heroic Thoughts", whether in an exercise or in published work. In answer to (c.ii) it assumes that the meaning is, not that the persons referred to *cannot do* the school exercises or poetic commonplaces, but that they are bad, 'no artists', at them (*artifices* heavily stressed in v.71 as *doctus* perhaps is at Hor. *S.* I.10.19). The parody-material is legitimately included because it illustrates an inept way of uttering Heroic Thoughts ('no artists at . . .'). It is not an example of a literary production which, in the case of the writers P. is criticising, does not exist because they cannot produce anything of that kind.

The above explanation is not easy or obvious, and the suggestions of G. L. Hendrickson (CP 23.1928.108-10) are worth considering: (e.g.) 'Look – we see Heroic Thoughts uttered by persons who *just now* were used to toying with Greek, who have *now* the art for the "Description of a Grove", the art, *now*, for "Praises of Rich Countryside" . . . etc.' (*modo*, 69, with *solitos*, 70; *nec . . . nec*, 70-1, corrected to *nunc . . . nunc*. Hend. also reads *videmus*, 'we see', for *docemus*, cf. n.22 above). This introduces the parody with better logic as a dreadful example of what these poets, equipped with their training, such as it is, can produce. However, the correction lacks MS evidence. The nearest parallels in P.'s MSS are perhaps at 1.36, 5.174.

It would also be possible to take vv.69-75 as a continuing part of "what the public says", viz. a boast that sublime material (cf. v.68) is being successfully produced by people who have not been practised in traditional poetic common-places or school-exercises. In this case either vv.70b-75 would indirectly cast scorn on the exercises or commonplaces as a means of approaching composition, showing, perhaps (see Appx. *A*. i) how their pastoral details intrude where true magnificence

is needed; or: vv.70b-72 might scorn the poetic commonplaces (school-exercises) a
comic and vv.73-5, 'Whence Remus ... plough home' might be an interruption by
showing, still by means of parody, how defective are the attempts at 'Heroic Thou
by 'persons used to toying with Greek', and in fact how full they are of mundane a
pastoral imagery although the writers are not practised in commonplaces (exercise
of countryside-description.

It is not necessarily an argument against this type of interpretation to say th
the opening words of the sentence (see (a) above) imply criticism of 'teaching
utterance of Heroic Thoughts to persons used to toying with Greek' and that there
fore they cannot be uttered by someone who favours just that teaching-process; fc
implicitly damaging admissions figure in the arguments of the interlocutor(s) else-
where in the poem, see Br p. 178, n. 5. Since in these last interpretations the
pastoral commonplaces (exercises) are unequivocally rejected, the assertion that
present-day writers cannot produce them combines perfectly naturally with the
parody of them (see c.iii above); and since they are now the main target of criticis
(c.i) and (c.ii) above cease to be a trouble. However, either of these interpretation
attributes to the interlocutor fair powers of criticism against (probably) current
school or poetic practice, which would be more typically attributed to P. in this
satire and elsewhere and would suit much less well his interlocutor-figure(s) of this
satire, uncritical admirer(s) of current practice.

Although it is impossible to be absolutely content with any of the above
interpretations it perhaps would not be disputed that P.'s general drift is to criticis
the lack of preparation of contemporaries, and possibly their methods of
preparation, for composition on grand themes. By contrast, in vv.76-8 P. may be
supposed to entertain either of two diametrically opposed views in a current litera
dispute (cf. the discussion of Br pp. 176-8), see item (d) below.

76-8

(a) Opinions vary upon the question whether these vv. are to be separated fr
or are to be part of the same utterance as the outcry *euge poeta*! ('Bravo, *so* poeti
v.75b. The cry is often taken as P.'s ironical applause for the "Rich-Countryside-
Cincinnatus" lines, 71b-5a − e.g. I.A.β* and all obelised versions below − but is nc
always taken in that way, e.g. I.B.β*, γ*, II.A.a* below); in the latter case they ar
the views they express concerning the old Latin tragedy-writers Accius and Pacuvi
would presumably form part of the reaction to the parody in the passage just discu
ed, vv.69-75. In the former case they would start a fresh (though possibly a relate
argument. In the list of alternatives under the headings I, II below an obelus deno
interpretations which would separate the outcry from vv.76-8, an asterisk denotes
those which would join the two and the presence of both signs denotes that both
possibilities are open.

(b) It would be helpful, though not perhaps essential, if the interpretation
chosen from all those available (see below) were such that vv.76-8 represented the

instruction, persuasion, warning or urging of some person or persons to take up literary views of some kind; because vv.79ff. include a reference to *hos monitus* (='these warnings, advice like this'; 'oracles like these') and to their results.

(c) The results of the 'oracles' are a *sartago* (? 'frypan', 80) of language, and opinions differ about the connotations of the word. Anc. Comm., Augustine (*Conf.* 3.1) and Isidore (*Orig.* 20.8.5) seem to connect it especially with the idea of *noise*, but it would be not unnatural to see it as a symbol of a mixture-of-contents should the context be found to favour that interpretation.

(d) vv.76-8 may be understood and punctuated in various ways, which form two groups with diametrically opposed tendencies, examples of which follow. (For the meaning of *, † see above, (a).)

I.   P. is implying or stating that in some degree or other *he disapproves of archaic literature,* perhaps, see (b) above, considered especially as a formative influence on modern writers.

A.   In Persius's mouth;
(a) a hostile statement or exclamation†, setting forth a further point in criticism of education or literature, the admiration of ancient models, 'There are people (so misguided as to be) drawn to a scrawny play of Accius or (Pacuvius's) warty Antiope ... (!)' So Cas, Ja, CN, Sciv., Rudd, Br p. 179, cf. Bo.
(β) an ironical statement *†, sarcastically recommending the use of Accius and Pacuvius as literary models, '(Bravo!) There are people who are drawn to ... scrawny ... Accius ... Pacuvius ... '

B.   In the mouth of an interlocutor (just anyone; or a member of the Public (v.63); or one of the 'bleary fathers' (v.79));
(a) a statement† defending modern literature against the previous imputation that it is unfitted for Heroic Writing, 'There *are* people with an admiration for scrawny ... Accius ... Pacuvius ... ' Suggested by Br, pp. 178-9.
(β) A statement*† advising the young to use Accius and Pacuvius as literary models, 'There *are* people who admire ... '
(γ) A regretful question*†, 'Is there *anyone* now who's drawn to ... ?'

II.   P. is implying or stating that in some degree or other *he approves of archaic literature,* perhaps, see (b) above, considered especially as a formative influence on modern writers.

A.   In the mouth of an interlocutor (defined as above, I.B);
(a) a hostile statement*† or exclamation*† or question*†, scornful of Accius and Pacuvius either in general or *by comparison with the 'excellence'

103

of the performance witnessed in vv.71b-5a, '(Bravo!) There are people now (Are there people . . . ?) who are (silly enough to be) drawn to Accius . . . Pacuvius . . . !' So (qn.†) Nisbet, Cl(?); (qn.*) VP, Hendrickson, CP 23. 1928.108f. (P. Thomas, *Mnemos.*, n.s., 49.1921.34-6, combines this last interpretation with the version above-mentioned of vv.69-75 whereby those vv. are a continuing part of 'what the Public says'. He regards the whole of v 63b-78 as laudatory appreciation of contemporary poets spoken by a quick succession of different interlocutors. The Public admires their skill (63-5). Comment is passed upon it by one of the Public's members (65b-66) and further speakers comment upon their ability at lofty satire (67f.), their capacity to tackle epic themes without training (69-75) and their superiority to Accius and Pacuvius (75b-78). *euge poeta* (see (a) above) is part of the last section; the section, however, is not a reaction to its predecessor, but, like all its predecessors, a random example of the kind of appreciation that might be heard at any recitation or meeting for literary discussion.)

(β) a reasoning question†, defending the moderns against P.'s attack, '*Is* anyone now drawn to . . . (an ancient mode of writing which, since you are displeased with the moderns, you seem to be advocating)?'

(γ) a question*† or statement*† or exclamation*†, sarcastic against the line of argument P. has been advancing in criticism of modern poetry, '(Bra (So) there is (Is there, then . . . ?) someone who's drawn to Accius . . . Pacuvius . . . !'

B.   In Persius's mouth;

(a) a scornful question*, as in II.A(a) but ironical, 'Bravo! (In face of such fine writing) could anyone now be drawn to . . . etc.?' So D.

(β) a statement† recommending the use of Accius and Pacuvius as literary models, 'There *are* people who admire . . . '

(γ) a regretful question†, 'Is there *anyone* now who's drawn to . . . ?' Cf. Bo.

Despite the evidence (Br p. 178 n.5 alluded to above) that P.'s interlocutor m; make damaging admissions even while earnestly arguing for his own views, it does n seem to me that any genuine admirer of Accius and Pacuvius could be made to refer to their works as *venosus* (scrawny) or *verrucosa* (warty), or to parody Pacuvius as damagingly as these lines do (cf. Appx. *A.* i). The examples Br quotes are much less obtrusive than this. Therefore I am inclined to eliminate I.B (a), (β), (γ), II.B (β), (γ) above.

Br argues firmly, pp. 174-9, that admiration for archaic literature existed and exerted influence upon writers in P.'s day, that it is unlikely that P. would speak in favour of Accius and Pacuvius, representatives of a genre traditionally abhorred by satirists (and cf. the further arguments of Rudd, CR, n.s., 21.1971.378), and that some version of the type represented in group I above, A(a), or perhaps B(a) should be chosen. I do not know if the second (and therefore the third) of these points has to be granted.

P. associates the type of writing to which he is opposed almost entirely with ideas of smoothness (vv.63-5, 92), weakness and delicate refinement (vv. 33-5, 65f., 85f., 98, 104-6) and effeminacy (vv.18-23, 81-2, 87, 98, 103-4). Passages can be quoted to show the admiration for the Ancients that existed in some quarters, but nearly all such passages (e.g. Sen. *Ep.* 114.13, Tac. *Dial.* 21-3, cf. 20, Mart. 11.90) speak of archaic elements as items making for *roughness* of style. Mart. 11.90 in particular is worth comparing. It attributes to its addressee a dislike for smooth style and a love of rough (vv.1-2, on which cf. n. 21, Sen. *Ep.* 114.15), and mockingly gives samples of such a style from the antique verbal forms and rough versification of Lucilius and Ennius, mentioning also the works of Accius and Pacuvius. It therefore seems to me that P., who has said that the Public has a love of smooth style (vv. 63-5) ought to be presenting the comments and quotations concerning the extreme roughness of Accius and Pacuvius as part of the popular view. The passage would then express itself against the Ancients very much as Martial does and the terms in which it argues would be thoroughly consistent with his (at v.96f. there may even be the type of sexual innuendo with which the Epigram closes, cf. Appx. *A.iii*) but it would express a view opposed to that of P. It would not be impossible, but it would be unexpected, if P. had mentioned Accius and Pacuvius, who were reputed among contemporaries (besides Martial, see Tac. *Dial.* 20.5, 21.7) to be rough stylists and to contribute to rough style in their admirers, as being poets admired by persons who cultivate a smooth style; and the more literally, i.e. the less ironically, or as some unfortunate admission of an interlocutor (see above, Br p.178 n.5), one takes the adjectives 'scrawny' (*venosus*) and 'warty' (*verrucosa*) applied to the works of Accius and Pacuvius, the more unexpected it would be. It would be unexpected too if P. had said (vv.81-2) that persons who admired or imitated or were advised to imitate Accius and Pacuvius so described (by whatever irony or mistake) wrote '*degraded* things that make the Smart Set's *hairless* limbs cavort . . .' (cf. vv.20-1, also 87, 103f. which seem aligned with 81-2); and the remarks about the scrawniness etc. of Accius and Pacuvius would most naturally represent the point of view put forward by v.92, which calls attention to the 'beauty and grace' that have now been 'added to *crude* metres', the point of view of the admirer of contemporary writing, the (fashionable) Public, cf. vv.63-6. Further, it would be possible that P. here satirises people who like the archaic authors Accius and Pacuvius while disliking Vergil's *Aeneid* and comparing it to an *old* stick (vv.96f.); and possible too that he is satirising two distinct groups, one of which wrongheadedly finds admirable the wartiness (etc.) of the antique Accius and Pacuvius whilst the other paradoxically despises the *Aeneid* as old and rough; but again it would probably be more natural to take it that he is aiming at a single group which dislikes both the antique Accius and Pacuvius for their roughness and outlandishly 'lofty' poetic vocabulary (cf. Appx.A.i) and the *Aeneid* because, they say, it is rough and antique. Cf. perhaps Sen. *Ep.* 114.13 who, discussing prose, lets us know incidentally that he holds no great opinion of orators of the first century B.C. (Crassus, Curio), while reserving his main condemnation for those who seek for models in more ancient times yet, and the not dissimilar sentiments involving Cicero and others, Tac. *Dial.* 21-3; also, on Vergil as archaist, Br p. 184 n.3.

In the passage immediately preceding vv.76-8 it is perhaps a permissible conclusion (cf. above, also n.22 and Appx. *A.i*) that P. has parodied the attempts of incompetent moderns (vv.70f.) to write in lofty style (vv.69, 73-5), a topic introduced during popular praise of modern poetry (v.68). The parody (cf. Appx. *A.i* seems not to betray the influence of archaic Latin tragedy, and there thus seems no especial reason for the subject of contemporary admiration of Accius and Pacuvius to be introduced either by Persius speaking against modern fashions (although — Br p. 179 — it could no doubt be introduced as a completely new subject of criticism or by an interlocutor speaking in favour of the adoption of archaic influences by contemporary authors. Whereas in view of the same piece of parody (again cf. Appx. *A.i*) there would be good motivation for a passage which, representing P.'s point of view, tended to disapprove, if not of the neglect, at least of the scornful dismissal of authors who, whatever their faults, were generally admitted (Hor. *Epl.* 2.1.56, 61-72) to have had some success in a heroic and dignified genre. It is true that the parody of Pacuvius (v.78, cf. Appx. *A.i*) justifies to an extent the hostile criticism of him and Accius which the lines contain. But the impression that one gets from Tac. *Dial.* 20.5, 21.7, Mart. 11.90.6 is that these two names were bywords in criticism of P.'s day against the Ancients, and the type of parody offered against Pacuvius here is the same to which he had been subjected as early as Lucilius (cf. n.24, Br p. 174, n.1; also Lucilius, Ennius at Mart. 11.90.4f.). It is, then, very possible that P. wrote vv.76-8 not as a comment of his own on Accius and Pacuvius but as an example of a trite and insensitive criticism of the Ancients, cf. the centurion and his 'popular caricature of the philosopher', 3.77ff.

I therefore feel free, and perhaps inclined, to adopt an interpretation from group II above, and have opted for the hostile question, II.A(*a*), linked with *euge poeta*! ('Bravo! *So* poetic!', 75b) to form a naively enthusiastic reception for P.'s ironical parody in the contemporary manner (P. 'We teach utterance of Heroic Thoughts to persons who are . . . no artists at the ingredients of such writing, for example . . .) Interlocutor: 'That's *very* good! Would anyone now be drawn to scrawny Accius . . . Pacuvius . . . ?' The rejection of famous but antiquated works by comparison with new ones is sufficiently apt, cf. Hendrickson op. cit. (above, p.104).

It is true that Lucilius (refs., Br p. 174 n.1) wrote parodies against the loftier writings of Accius, Pacuvius and Ennius (who were in some measure his contemporaries); it is true that Horace argued against those who admired Lucilius "right or wrong" (*S.* 1.10) and that he pleaded for recognition of the virtues of modern poetry (including epic and tragedy, *S.* 1.10.42-4) and against a bigoted preference for ancient writers in general, though not without implying that the latter had virtues (*S.* 1.4.60-2, *Epl.* 2.1.64-70, 73f.) and that preference for the former must be based on genuine virtues of its own (ib. 76f.). It is true that P. elsewhere makes fun and parody of Ennius's epic (6.10f.) and of contemporary epic and tragedy (1.4 and 50, with Appx. *A.i* p.98, 5.1-4, 8f., 11-13, 17-20). However, P.'s prologue (cf. Prol. and nn., esp. n.1) and the general tendency of this satire (see above) suggest that, whatever Horace for example may have had to say (with qualifications, cf. above) in favour of the moderns and against persons who (in accord with prevailing fashion?) favoured the ancients, Persius, facing a different situation (cf. Wimmel, quoted Prol. n.1) and quite possibly with different critical predispositions, felt impelled to attack a different target — a fashionable modernism which over-valued stylistic qualities of smoothness and refinement; and it would not be inconsistent with this should he have felt that the abhorrence of his contemporaries for old-fashioned roughnesses found in works and traditions of literature which they despised led them to under-value certain necessary virtues which those works and traditions exemplified (cf., perhaps, Quint. *Inst.* 2.5.21-3).

If this suggestion about P.'s intentions is correct, the view put forward in this satire is distinct alike from that found in the poems of Martial, which use both effeminacy (2.86.4-5) and rough Accius-and-Pacuvius masculinity (11.90) as symbols of different types of poem which displease him, and from that of Pliny who perhaps saw refinement in works that others might have called over-refined and effeminate, *Ep.* 4.27.1, 5.17.2, (both of which include reference to sublimity achieved by poets of refined style), 5.3.2 ctr. Mart. 2.86.2, 7.4.6 vv.8ff., and who also found acceptable the imitation of ancient authors (*Ep.* 1.16.5f., 6.21.2, 4). There would be especial opposition between vv.76-8 and Martial 11.90, but that need not preclude us from thinking that, when discussing the type of poets that forms the subject of Sat. 1, P. was capable of implying approval of Accius and Pacuvius (or at least disapproval of scornful neglect of them) or that there was something valuable in what he says. In another context (see above) he may parody epic or tragedy, contemporary or ancient; but perhaps we should guard against thinking even so that he was without qualification the enemy of the ancient or the lofty any more than Horace's critical writing shows him to have been. Juvenal decries a mass of contemporary verse, including tragic and epic materials (Sat. 1.2-11) but he seems not ill-disposed to Statius's *Thebaid* (7.82-6) or Lucan (7.79).

In fact it is not clear that P. does entirely avoid or discourage the use of high style or the admiration of antique authors. Line 1 of this poem, redolent whether of Lucilius or of Lucretius (cf. n.2) is in high style. Seemingly he approves of it, and both Lucilius and Lucretius are mentioned by contemporaries (Tac. *Dial.* 23.2, Mart. 11.90.4) as authors in favour with persons of archaic tastes. The line contains two elisions. Villeneuve (VP p. LVI cf. VE p. 208) points out the relative frequency of elision in P., not least in Sat. 1, and the contrast it offers there to the rare or non-existent elision of P.'s 'citations', cf. Appx. *A*(i) p.99. Probably elision is one of the 'masculine' features of old poetry that are criticised in Martial's quotation of Lucilius (11.90.4, cf.8), and P.'s general views clearly favour masculinity and reject its opposite. He may have felt that it was a feature that the stylistic traditions of satire especially offered. At Sat. 6.9 a line of Ennius beginning with an archaism *Lunai* (see Bailey on Lucretius, vol. I, pp. 75-7) is quoted, seemingly with appreciation. A further feature of the line (although it may come from a satire, see n.6 ad loc.) is its declamatory ring. Persius, 1.123f., 2.61, 3.35-8, 66-72, 5.34-42, 63-5, 6.2-6 and (despite some irony, still with a basically serious intent) 5.141f., 152f. do not lack a certain exaltation such as Lucilius also could achieve on occasion.

Despite the criticism and parody of contemporary epic and tragedy at the beginning of Sat.5 and the description of his own style as 'following the talk of the streets' (5.14 cf. Br p.3, W. S. Anderson WZUR 15.1966.410, 414f.) one would hesitate to describe P.'s overall style with the phrase 'akin to the colloquial' (*sermoni propiora*) applied by Horace *S.* 1.4.42 to his own satire and I think that at 5.21, 26 ('at the Muse's command', 'I may require twice-fifty throats'), with all allowances made for irony, P. insists on being allowed to use such exaltation of style as this or that subject may make appropriate. The general context and especially the metaphor in vv.24f. where Cornutus is invited to test his words for sincerity to see 'what rings solid, what's stucco of a painted tongue' must mean that P. thinks of his words (here at least and arguably elsewhere) as having a certain elegance, of a dignified kind (cf. 26), and that it is possible, in his opinion, for such elegance and dignity of language to have solid meaning and worth.

A further conclusion which could be drawn from this part of Sat. 5 (vv.21-9) is that in P.'s view what would justify elegance and dignity in an author's style is the having something significant to say, so that dignity of style does appropriate honour to, and is well-supported by, content. Martial 10.4.7f., 10 rejects the 'vain twaddle' of sundry mythological themes, including those of Oedipus and *Thyestes* (cf. 5.7,17f., nn. 4,7). He associates them all with Callimachean poetry (v.12, with which cf. Pers. 1.134), cf. Appx. *A(i)* p. 97 above, and commends his own verse: "Read this, of which Life can say, 'It is my own' . . . it is of man that my page savours". In the early verses of Sat. 5 and in Sat. 1 P. may be expressing a similar and similarly-caused dissatisfaction with contemporary poetry, not least (vv.14, 68ff.) where it aspires to grandeur. An allied theme, 1.83-91, is the employment of the wrong kind of stylistic ornament where Life offered the right kind of content.

Clearly if one chooses a version of vv.76-8 according to which P. is implying some approval of archaic poets or those who admire them (Group II above) it is not possible to take *sartago* (see (c) above) in the sense of a mixture of antique and modern elements of diction or versification, because the people to whom P. is opposed reject, in one way or another, the influence of Accius and Pacuvius. It is possible, in view of the ancient evidence, to insist that *sartago* is a metaphor of spitting, sizzling etc., implying e.g. cheap noise, a style that is sordid although verbose because its authors have neglected to study ancient tragedy. But the parody of 71-5 could be described as a mixture in that both it is full of assorted rural components (71-2) and these humble and prosaic items combine (73-5) in an unholy because inappropriately-handled, mish-mash with images of Old Roman Heroism.

All interpretations in Group I above give good or satisfactory sense-connection of the type desired in (b) above, with the following *hos monitus*, except for A(*a*), In Group II, interpretations B(*β*) and (*γ*) yield no good connections with *hos monitus*. B(*a*) yields one that is tolerable only; A(*a-γ*) yield good connections.

(iii)   On Imagery and Sexual Double-Entendre

In the matter of double-entendres, especially sexual ones, my imagination and in my experience that of others too, easily reacts to words which originally had no ulterior purpose, and it is clear that a reader's or hearer's reaction may be more informative about his or her imagination than about a poet's intention. Nevertheless, decisions to hear or not to hear sexual double-entendres in this poem must be faced because (see text below) M. Coffey's remark that "Persius Sat. 1 is not innocent literature" is true and because in virtue of the emotion-loaded nature of the subject, the decisions make a good deal of difference to an interpretation of the poem and to our view of its author. Ultimately the responsibility can only rest upon each informed reader. I have confined discussion of the subject to an appendix to (so far as possible) avoid prejudicing a reader's first acquaintance with the passages discussed by others or by me. I have tried to govern my suggestions in the essay which follows by asking whether puzzles exist in interpreting a passage and, if they do, whether the assumption of a deliberately created sexual double-entendre would help to explain them.

Features of the imagery in this satire (ears, expressions of applause, heroic images, disease, dress and appearance, homosexuality, effeminacy, impotence, old age, food and drink) are closely discussed by Br, ch. 3, 4, and there are treatments also by Dessen pp. 32-8 and (interspersed within commentary) by Korzeniewski; also (of selected images) by K. J. Reckford, *Hermes* 90.1962.476-83 and W. J. N. Rudd, CR (n.s.) 20.1970.282-5. Cf. also M. Coffey, art. cit. below, p. 190. Br concentrates a good deal upon a search for innuendo which would make more pervasive in the poem a strand of hostile judgements in which P. taints contemporary poetry by associating it with images of perverted sex and lack of masculinity (e.g. vv. 18-21, 87, 103). One might not wish to deny that vv.81-2 (where vv.20-1 are readily recalled), v.98 (cf. n.31) and perhaps 'shaved' in v.85 impart some taint of sexual disgrace to the compositions discussed in those places; or, perhaps, that the attire of the reciter at v.32 would, together with the subject and the unpleasing features of his performance, rouse some doubts about his masculinity; but details of Br's interpretations are open to doubt or discussion (cf. reviews of G. B. Townend JRS 66.1976.269f., M. Coffey CR (n.s.) 26.1976.189-91, W. Clausen, *Gnomon* 49.1977.311-13).

In two further passages it might, I think, be urged that to recognise a covert sexual reference helps to give a more thorough or a more reasonable explanation of the sense than would otherwise exist:

(a)   *V.25 (24-7).* V. Buchheit, Rh.M.103.1960.218-22 (cf. also his preceding arguments) shows persuasively that in P.'s contemporary Martial (4.52.2) 'wild fig-tree' (*caprificus*) is part of a scheme of sexual slang-imagery and denotes a penis (especially as erect). If we understand the use of the word here as a double-entendre intentionally created by P., the Interlocutor, who speaks of the power of his inspiration through the metaphors of a ferment and of a wild fig-tree (vv. 24-5), unintentionally makes what could be construed as an admission (see above p.102, Br p. 178, n.5) that a sexual need precedes or accompanies the recitation of (his) verse and that reciting it is a sexual act. Since P's sexual images include that of an audience undergoing passive homosexual intercourse with poems ('trembling verse')

109

performing the active rôle (vv.19-23), the double-entendre would be not inappropri: It is also worth notice that P.'s reaction to what the Interlocutor says is strongly moralistic. He takes it as removing or penetrating a mask of severity (*senium;* Rudd, op. cit., p. 282) and exclaims '*o mores!*'. It is possible, but a little unnatural, to imagine that a simple inability to see a purpose for education, unless it issues in literary production and performance, might be viewed as so terribly perverse and so typical of modern views as to call forth a curse upon modern morals; and the mask « affected gravity which is thus penetrated *might* be the apparently serious artistic intent with which contemporaries compose poetry (vv.13ff.). Nevertheless moral sternness is a well-established connotation of *senium* (LS, cf. esp. Sen. *Hippol.* 917ff., B on 6.16) and the idea of old age, the literal meaning of the word, was last found associated with *patrui* which has that same connotation (vv.9-11 with n.5, Br p. 142; Rudd, op. cit.). It would, then, be natural — more natural — to view the Interlocutor's utterance, vv.24-5, as capable of throwing some serious moral (as opposed to serious intellectual) blame upon the Interlocutor or the performance of which he speaks.

The second part of P.'s response: *usque adeone // scire tuum nihil est nisi te scire hoc sciat alter?* (vv.26f.) is usually interpreted (e.g.), 'Is your knowledge so worthless unless someone knows that you know (i.e. have) it?', cf. CN. This meets, but meets somewhat obliquely, the point made by the Interlocutor. He has said: 'What is the use of study unless it issues in the public utterance of one's sentiments?' Since the study he is primarily thinking of must surely be rhetorical study, his point is fair so far as it goes; rhetoric has little or no use except as a performing art. P.'s answer could be a deliberate refusal to see or to meet this point: it is equivalent to: 'Knowledge is sufficient in itself', an apparently unexceptionable statement which disregards or perhaps deliberately belittles the peculiar nature and aim of the Study referred to by the Interlocutor. On the other hand a more direct answer results if we take *hoc,* object of *scire* in v.27, not as something vague, ' . . . that you know *a thing*' (cf. TLL *hic* 2737.2-29) but as a direct reference to the previous speech of the Interlocutor. Then we might interpret: 'Does knowing (of any kind, but includi: the rhetorical skill to which you refer) have so little worth unless someone else know that you know this?' — i.e., that you know the art of reciting in such a way that your performance constitutes (merely) a release for powerful pent-up enthusiasm, o else in such a way that the performance becomes a sexual instrument experienced b· the listener; P. has in mind both possibilities of the image *caprificus,* but it is the Martialian one which calls forth the strong moral condemnation (see earlier). The public exhibition of either facet of the reciter's art is, he says, unnecessary and unbecoming.

(b)   At vv.96f. the assumption of a sexual double-entendre could help to explain what is at first sight a rather odd choice of image — the cork-tree branch.

In view of the other applications of sexual and homosexual images to literature, including those at vv.87, 98 (cf. n.31), 103, it is probably worth commen: ing in any case on the masculine associations of the first two words of the *Aeneid,*

110

which the Interlocutor quotes as the title of a work (cf. n.29) that he despises. In the remainder of the sentence the images used of the *Aeneid*, 'surely it's (?)spongy and thick-barked like an old stick dried out with stunted cork', though not inappropriate, do seem to be among the more arbitrary of P.'s images in their degree of likeness to what they are used to describe, namely a work of poetic literature. None of them, unlike other images used of poetry by P. (see below), suggests a link with the idea, 'poem', by having associated with it notions like blasts of wind or ingestion or psychosomatic effect which are conventionally or fairly naturally associated with poetry or its reception by an audience. It might be worth noting additionally, concerning the two words of the Vergil-title, that *vir* can mean 'virility' (Lucan 10.134; Cat. 63.6, Ellis, Kroll ad loc.) and that *arma* can be used to refer to the penis — 'equipment', 'weapon' (TLL s.v., 601.58f.; only in poems about Priapus, but this must surely be an accident of survival in view of the uses of *hasta, telum,* ὅπλον in this sense). This would be a wicked thrust for P. to have permitted the opponent, his creation (v.44), to deliver. Nevertheless it is not essentially more hostile to Vergil than the ordinarily-accepted interpretation of this v., and if it is true (see Appx. *A.ii*) that vv.76-8 are words of an opponent, it is not foreign to the manner of the poem in its use of quotation from old-style works to ridicule them (v.1, q.v. with n.2, may be a further instance of such ridicule). Nor would it differ, in the extent of the licence and pithiness of argument granted to the opponent, from 3.78-85, 5.190-1. Its play with the physical and literary notions of 'virility' would have some parallel at Mart. 11.90.8. It is not without wit, and it would make P.'s choice of the imagery which follows much less arbitrary. P., who in Sat. 5.5-13 talks of poetry as food or as blasts of air, at least once in this poem speaks of a poem as if it were a penis (vv.20f.; on v.25 see above), and in vv.81f, 87 the use of the same image concerning a prose oration is probably implied. Nothing makes it impossible to think that P. would allow his opponent to use this type of image in reply to the satirist's uses of it and his criticisms of modern poetry's effeminacy — to say, in fact, that *arma virum,* the phrase used as a title for the *Aeneid,* is, if suitably understood, the very name of the masculine organ; but that, in view of the rough and inflated style of the *Aeneid,* the weapons-and-manhood, the penis, which serves as its title, should be visualised as having unprepossessing characteristics, (?) an insubstantial sponginess ('puffy', *spumosum,* cf. Ja) and a rough, thick skin ('gnarled, fat', lit. 'with fat bark (or rind)'), like those of an *aged, withered cork-stick.* At the same time it would be shown how easily P.'s opponent accepts the view, elsewhere attributed to him by P. (see above), that some form of sexual stimulation is a function of literature and one criterion of its success; for his use of the simile of an ugly male organ to describe the *Aeneid*'s ugliness would imply that one source of his distaste for it was its inability to produce the type of sexual effects that is popular with contemporary audiences.

There is bibliographical information on interpretations of this Satire in D, p.140. Add Kugler, pp. 79ff., N. Rudd, CR 20.1970.286ff.

Most edd. (e.g. Ja, CN, Nem., VP, D, Sciv., Bo) believe that P. has no dramatic rôle in the opening scene (vv.1-14) of the poem and that it is some other person who is woken by the Friend. In this case the first persons plural (vv.3, 12, 14) are interpreted as only ironically inclusive of the speaker (cf. 1.13, 104), and the first person singular 'I explode' (*findor*, v.9) as an exclamation. The first half of the Satire as it usually appears may be summarised:

1-7 FRIEND: Here we are snoring in bed at this hour. Disgraceful! (G. L. Hendrickson, CP 23.1928.333f. argues that the first sentence means, e.g. "So *this* is what you're constantly engaged in!" and that the rest of the scene up to v.4 ' . . . five times met.' is scene-setting narration by the poet. Similarly Bo gives the whole c vv.1-4 to the poet.)

7-9 YOUNG STUDENT: Is it so late? Come, slaves! I'm furious (*findor*)!

10-14 Young Student's activities (noticed already, 8b, 9b) further described b; Persius.

15-62 (with a brief interruption, v.19a). Poet's lecture, addressed to the Youn; Student, on laziness and neglect of philosophy. (Sciv. makes the Friend lecture as fa as v.34, VP as far as v.62, Nem. to v.118.)

A. E. Housman, CQ 7.1913.16-18 (*Classical Papers* II, pp. 850f.) powerfully criticises the type of interpretation of vv.1-14 contained in the above. I follow C1 in adopting his version of that passage. (Rudd, following Hendrickson (above), gives th first sentence to the Friend; and he gives vv.15-16a to Persius's SELF, bewailing his lot and luck.)

From vv.63ff. the lecture tends towards the tone and content of a public sermon (cf. D p. 137, VP p. 85). Housman (p. 18/851) believes that vv.15-62 are an address of P.'s higher nature to his lower (which has a half-line riposte at v.19a) and that at 63ff. "he turns from himself to the public"; and he points out that the theme of 63ff. is different: " . . . no longer those who sin against light and knowledge" (cf. vv.52-7) "but those who sit in darkness unilluminated by philosophy". D would have the address to the individual, the young student (see above), continue as far as v.76.

I have argued (*Latomus* 32.1973.537-9, 545f.) that there is some reason for regarding vv.73-6, and good reason for regarding vv.107-18, as indications that the lecture, whatever its style and content, continues to be uttered to, or for the benefit of, its original auditor; and that it is not unnatural to think that it is the Friend, rath than P., who gives it. I also think (cf. art. cit. pp. 540f.) that vv.45f., 53-5 contain material that is most naturally interpreted as hostile to the Stoa (cf. the translation b Rudd of the latter passage; although, as will be seen, I find the reference to the Stoa more, and the reference to its students less, sarcastic than he does) and as the view and the words of a speaker opposed to the Satire's generally Stoic argument. I have therefore chosen to take vv.44-62 not as a united lecturing-passage (e.g. 'I wasted my time at school; why not? My aims were those of a child; but you, being Stoic-traine should not waste yours', cf. Ja, CN, N. Rudd CR 20.1970.287) but as a dialogue in which are discussed: inclination and training; excuses based upon them; and the general aims of life to which they relate. P: 'Catonian utterances' (cf. the moral writings that no doubt were to have been his subject of study at v.10ff.; possibly also the improving remarks of his Friend) 'were a boring subject that I avoided attending to at school.' F: 'That's understandable: your[1] interests were (as yet) those of childhood.' P: 'You were especially equipped for moral analysis' (cf. the Friend's remarks both in general and most recently about P.'s schoolday pursuits) 'by the lessons of the Daubed Stoa.' F: 'You have beheld the Moral Vision . . . have you (still) no aim in view?'

The *prima facie* inconsistency of vv. 58-9 (see Rudd, art. cit. p. 287 and n. 1) is much more obvious in a situation where the person addressed has been speaking immediately previously; however, it seems resolved by the rendering in the text, which takes the verbs *stertis, oscitat* quite generally and not as denoting an action that is taking place at that very minute. Since snoring and yawning are not usually simultaneous conditions of somnolence, this in any case seems the likeliest interpretation. For the 'adversative' use of *adhuc*, 'still', see TLL s.v., 657.46-54, 57-9. The sentence may hint at or exclusively denote the 'sleep' of spiritual unawareness, cf. Sen. *Ep.* 53.8 (also 36.9), Hor. *Epl.* 1.2.33, KH ad loc., *Sat. Sulpiciae* (Baehrens PLM, vol. V, pp. 93ff.) v.56, Epict. *Diss.* 1.20.11. It may also be taken as a reproving question, cf. *Latomus* art. cit. p. 546. Whatever interpretation of the passage as a whole be adopted, some contrast seems possible or likely between the sleeper in these lines and the 'young men . . . sleepless and intent' of v. 54f.

Such a version additionally brings the themes of vv. 1-62 and 63-118 more nearly into harmony. The auditor in this case is not a sinner against the light (Housman) but a very new and imperfect aspirant to Stoic studies (cf. vv.21-3, 11-14). He listens to an exhortation to philosophise which, though the first part is more particularly addressed to his case, is all equally applicable to it.

Hor. *S.* 2.3 and 2.7 are more naturalistically arranged and in neither of them does the auditor interrupt in the middle of the lecture. Nevertheless, these satt. could have suggested the kind of arrangement I propose. If it can be accepted, more unity may be discovered in the Satire than Ja (p. 143) or D (p. 140) allows. See further W. S. Smith Jr., 'Speakers in the Third Sat. of P.', CJ 64.1969.305-8, whose proposals, which I first read after 1973, are of the same general type.

---

1. This is a possible rendering, despite '*My* aims' in the summary of Ja, CN, Rudd given above. P's mode of expression dispenses with personal pronouns, as Latin often does, and his main verbal expression, *erat in voto* (v.49), is third personal: 'This or that form of knowledge (sixes, the narrow pot's neck, etc.) was the subject of (my? your?) heart's desire'.

Appendix C, Satire 4

This Satire is usually interpreted and punctuated so that the interview between Socrates and Alcibiades forms only the introduction and the Poet speaks as preacher from v.23 onwards (except for a small interruption by an Interlocutor, vv.46f.), moralising on the subject of self-awareness. Ramsay, for instance, gives the following summary of this section (p. 357; extra line-references have been inserted): 'Not one of us has any knowledge of himself, though we are all ready to discourse about our neighbours (vv.23-4). Ask a question about Vettidius, and you will learn . . .how miserly he is, how he starves alike himself and his slaves (vv. 25-32). And are you any better, though your vices lie in an opposite direction . . . ? (vv.33-41).

Thus we lash and are lashed in turn. Do not deceive yourself; however much the neighbourhood may praise you . . . Look carefully into your own heart, and acknowledge how poorly you are furnished (vv.42-52).'

This is a reasonably close reflection of the interpretations of Ja, VP, and (?) CN. It is somewhat less close to those of Nem., D, Sciv., Bo, but still shows similarities.

The central section, vv.23-43, presents problems. Vv.23f., 'We have no knowledge of ourselves, though ready to discourse about our neighbours', and vv.42f., 'We lash and are lashed in turn', seem naturally to be taken respectively as introduction to and recapitulation of (cf. Ramsay's 'Thus . . . ') the two examples which intervene between them. Accordingly one would expect the examples (a) to concern themselves with our neglect of our own faults and preference for criticising those of others cf. vv.23f.; and (b) to contain instantiation in which someone who criticises also suffers, or risks suffering, criticism himself, cf. vv.42f.

The problems have to do with the design of the examples:

1. It is very badly equipped to produce a sense which would accord with (b) above. It is hard to believe that the man criticised in the second example is the same as the man who utters criticism in the first, because, like the subject of the first example, he is addressed as 'you' and this leads us to expect that the two are identified or in principle identifiable. Yet the subject of the first example is *the* person who cannot utter criticism because he is instead its audience (cf. 'you will learn . . . '). Ja cures the situation by deciding (pp. 167, 175) that the subject of the second example, vv.33-41, is to be identified with the actual critic who answers the question about Vettidius in the first example; but this is the opposite of what we expect. VP (p. 97) believing, more naturally, that it is the listener in the first example who is criticised in the second, supposes that the former listens 'avec complaisance' to the criticism against Vettidius; so that, having to that extent shared in it, he can then be criticised in turn; but 'avec complaisance' has no warrant in the poem itself. Either version is reflected by Ramsay's phrase, 'And are you any better . . . ?' Neither is encouraged by the text.

2. The first example could be a suitable illustration of the theme (cf. (a) above) of criticism of others which leads to neglect of one's own faults. However, concerning the second there is every reason (*pace* the hints of Ja p. 167, Nem. p. 226, D p. 184

114

Sciv. p. 91, Bo p. 77) to believe that the criticism it contains is a true, because an eye-witness (cf. vv.34-8) account of something which is happening; and that, if true, it is in P.'s opinion a piece of merited, even necessary criticism; cf. his attitude to effeminacy in Sat. 1 and the reference to sunbathing, v.33, which has been slightingly referred to by P.'s hero, the 'bearded Master' at v.18. There must, then, be far less emphasis here, if any at all, on the idea of forgetting one's own faults whilst criticising others. In the circumstances it is hard to blame the 'stranger', or to suppose that P. would blame him, for uttering his criticisms, and hard to discern the idea of the stranger's faults being ignored; and there is consequent doubt about what purpose the second example serves and how it fits into its context. There is the possibility (cf. Ja, VP, Ramsay above) that it is being shown that *genuine and unpleasant* faults exist in the critic or the complaisant listener of the first example and that thus the lesson of vv.23f. is being driven home, but:

(i)   the text discourages such an interpretation, see above, (1).

(ii)   there is some oddity about the use of a stranger-*critic* for the purpose of passing valid judgement upon someone, since that critic's proper business, in the light of vv.23f., is to direct his attention within himself rather than elsewhere.

(iii)   it is also curious that the course of the argument presupposed by this interpretation should be impartially and detachedly summed up in vv.42f. very much as if the second case of criticism were as valid or as invalid, and of as much and as little concern, as the first; whereas (surely?) there is emphasis on the second case: 'you criticise others, but in fact you are sorely at fault yourself'.

Cf. the discussion of Kugler, pp.63ff., whose main conclusions, however, are very different from mine, and the remarks of Sciv. on '25-32', '33-41', '42-43'; also CN on v.25.

Finally, as in Sat. 3 (see Appendix B) and as Ja (cf. p. 167) recognises, there are reasons for thinking that the person addressed in vv.46-52 should be the auditor of the introductory passage (i.e. Alcibiades).

The version presented in the text above attempts to take account of these phenomena and also of some minor difficulties of sequence in vv.42-4, cf. *Latomus* 32.1973.521-34. The succeeding of Athenian by Roman 'scenery' should be no obstacle to it, as in fact the mixture already occurs at v.8, *Quirites*. It is not in any case unduly alarming; but P. may have had the purpose of 'up-dating', by the irrational juxtaposition, a long tradition of philosophical writing (cf. Dessen in n.1), to show that the things which take place between ancient figures represented in the tradition are not divorced from contemporary life.

According to many (see summaries of Ja, D, Bo) the Heir is virtually the only interlocutor in the Satire, the objections at vv.27ff., 33ff. being rhetorical, raised by the Satirist: 'But (you will say) . . . '; and the Satirist's conversation with the Heir, a face-to-face encounter, continues to, or nearly to, the end, where the final six lines discuss scornfully, either with him or with some new interlocutor, the insatiable lust for gain associated with his attitude.

I have preferred in general to follow B's interpretation, a main feature of which is that the argument with the Heir (vv.41b-68a) is parenthetic, being imagined by the Satirist *solely to illustrate* to an Objector, speaker of 33bff. (as of 27ff.), the Satirist's meaning, namely that an heir is powerless to influence a testator's use of his money during life. *Direct* address to the Objector, who throughout remains the Satirist's only real partner-in-dialogue, resumes at 69b: 'Is my Sunday . . . etc.?'

This interpretation fits more naturally Persius' distribution of second and third persons in vv.69b-74 and B's explanation of a slight difficulty in the second person *curtaveris* ('you've stunted . . . ') in v.34 seems adequate.

For the possibility, emphasised by many, that the end of the Satire might have been different, and even lengthily extended, had P. lived, see n.28; but the idea of insatiable greed (vv.75ff.) is as easily associable with an opponent of the philosophy of Utilization as is the idea of miserly economy (cf. Hor. *S.* 1.1.37-44, 62 . . . 65 . . . 73 . . . 92 . . . 96-7); and, whatever the truth was, P.'s editors could feel that the Satire had at least the appearance of completeness.

The argument of the central section, especially the 'Colonel Beestlie' (Bestius)-passage, vv.37b-40 presents other points for discussion:

(a)   The words ' . . . you've stunted the estate . . . ' and ' "Reduce the property . . . ?" ' suggest that the objection concerning the Heir (vv.33b-37a) stands as part of the same argument as, and in logical sequence after, the objection about the shipwrecked friend (vv.27-31a), help to whom was to be given by 'breaking a piece from *your green holdings*', vv.31f. The Heir is made to object to the spending of capital (see B p. 58) specifically. It is possible but less likely that the objection is a new and independent one against the spending of income that was recommended at vv.25f.

(b)   Against B (pp.62-4) and in the light of Bennett I p. 466 I think it probable that *tune bona incolumis minuas?* (v.37a) is an indignant question spoken by the Heir, 'Reduce the property, would you?' rather than a doubting, monitory question spoken by the Objector (or rhetorically-objecting Satirist): ' . . . Would you reduce the property when you've suffered no loss?' See also n.14 and B pp.64-5.

(c)   B's reasons, p. 78f., for taking *haec . . . metuas* (v.41a) as a question and not as a statement: 'That would worry you . . . ' seem good ones.

(d)   The Bestius-passage, which seems something of an intrusion into the argument (see (a-γ) below).

The critical remarks quoted in this passage, ' . . . that's how, since this gelded etc.' are usually interpreted as meaning that, thanks to the arrival of Greek Philosophy among the Romans, luxury has invaded farmhands, the lowest classes; therefore *a fortiori*, we take it, the Testator and the rest of Roman society are luxury's victims — cf. Housman CQ 7.1913.27 (*Classical Papers* II, p. 861), '*even* hedgers and ditchers' — and this leads to the squandering of resources.

Perhaps (see n.15) a second possibility can be maintained: the complaint might be that farmhands *as such* have gotten an unhealthy taste for some civilised addition to bare gruel or porridge (which makes them expensive to feed; farmhands (lit. 'hay-mowers', *faenisecae*) were likely to be slaves, Colum. 11.2.40 cf. 11.2.1, 11.1.3-9, 1.9.7ff., K. D. White, *Roman Farming,* London, 1970, p. 349). The complaint would then exemplify the attitude of the miserly owner of an estate who complains about expenses which any civilised farmer would be expected to bear, an attitude which the diet of Vettidius' slaves (4.31) is also probably intended to exemplify. According to this interpretation, as according to the more orthodox one, Bestius' censure of the Greeks would no doubt concern the importation of luxuries under the supposed influence of the Greek educators — or rather it associates the two by implying that this 'taste for learning' is a further imported luxury; but in this case it would additionally be aimed at the teachings of Greek philosophers to the effect that men have standing obligations to all other men (cf. Sat. 3.70-2) including slaves (Pohlenz I.136, 316, Sen. *Ep.* 47).

I am inclined to think that the latter interpretation has the greater point. It gives, in the context (see (a)), the more meaningful reason for the complainant's wrath against philosophers, and it touches, or continues to touch (as its rival does not), upon a philosophical point which P. would think worth airing. My view would be that the passage sets a complaint, from someone who objects to the expense of performing a basic and continuing obligation towards his employees or dependants, in a relationship of some kind with the attitude of someone (vv.27ff., 33ff.) who hesitates about the expense of performing a single obligation to a friend.

Speech-distribution and syntax of the passage are variously interpreted: (i) it may be an ordinary part of the Objector's (or Satirist's) warning: "(If you spend your substance) your heir will neglect . . . and Col. Beestlie, too, criticises Grecian education . . ." (Ja, CN); (ii) it may be a further part of a threatening speech of the Heir: " 'Reduce the property, would you? Col. Beestlie, too, criticises . . . ' " (Buecheler, Sciv.); or (iii) it may be translated, e.g. "Your heir will neglect . . . 'Reduce . . . would you?' and, *like Col. Beestlie* he criticises Grecian education: 'That's how . . . seasonings.' " (*Bestius* in apposition to the subject of the sentence, i.e. *heres*), so that the complaint 'That's how . . . etc.' , is a speech of *the Heir.*

All these versions are possible, and (iii) has a pleasingly neat and allusive construction (see C1 on v.37). Nevertheless all have the slight oddity that the Bestius-passage (although introducing new considerations) bases its objection on a case of exaggerated and irrational criticism and consequently scarcely deserves an answer, cf. above and B pp. 78, 79f.; and yet it is placed: (*a*) after an objection that has a certain degree of *prima facie* seriousness (the stinted funeral), the effect of which is consequently blunted, (β) in such a position as to give the impression that 41a, 'Would that worry you . . . etc.?' answers it especially, and (γ) so as to interpose a long distance between that answer and the objection (concerning your Heir's anger (37a) and consequent stinting of your funeral) which it answers most directly and successfully.

I have preferred, as minimising or removing these oddities (iv) an interpretation listed by VE pp. 340f., according to which the Bestius-passage is itself part of the answer to the objection of the stinted funeral and your Heir's anger. The Satirist himself presents Bestius and his complaint ironically as a parallel case to the Heir's angry resentment, and by its 'caricature'-content he criticises the basis of the Heir's feelings (and therefore the basis of the objection in which the Heir figures, and also of its fair-seeming predecessor (27ff.) which it presupposes, cf. (a) above) as a mean, Bestius-like philistinism. 'Would that worry you beyond cremation?' can naturally enough, if we wish, be a direct answer to the Bestius-passage which is not, upon this interpretation, a thing-in-itself but is a symbol or substitute for the Heir's stinting of Persius's funeral and the resentment that went with it; although equally the question may refer back directly to the original objection, the Bestius-passage being regarded as a parenthesis.

For discussion of the Satire's argument in general and in particular see B on vv.25-80, 31, 37a, 37b (esp. n.10), 41a, b, 42, 51 (*inquis*), 68, 71, 75ff. On the Bestius-passage see VE pp. 339-41.

Appendix E, The Ancient Life of Persius

The accounts of the life of Persius which appear in the editions and in other essays on his work are founded mainly upon a collection of biographical notes which is attached to a number of his manuscripts. Although there are difficulties concerning the origins and authorship of this work and the state of its text, it nevertheless is probably reliable in the main (cf. Ja p. III, VP pp. IV-XI, esp. X, Coffey p. 235 n.9). The information it contains on P.'s birth, family, teachers, friends and habits of composition have been commented on by (for example) Ja pp. IIIff., VE pp. 1ff. I offer a translation from the text of C1 (pp. 37ff.), using the notes of VP (pp.3ff.) and Bo (pp.1ff.).

VITA AULIS PERSI FLACCI DE COMMENTARIO PROBI VALERI SUBLATA

AVLES PERSIVS FLACCVS natus est pridie Non. Dec.
Fabio Persico L. Vitellio coss., decessit VIII Kal.
Dec. P. Mario Afinio Gallo coss.
   natus in Etruria Volaterris, eques Romanus, sanguine et
5 affinitate primi ordinis viris coniunctus. decessit ad octa-
vum miliarium via Appia in praediis suis.
   pater eum Flaccus pupillum reliquit moriens annorum
fere VI. Fulvia Sisennia nupsit postea Fusio equiti Romano
et eum quoque extulit intra paucos annos.
10   studuit Flaccus usque ad annum XII aetatis suae Vola-
terris, inde Romae apud grammaticum Remmium Palae-
monem et apud rhetorem Verginium Flavum. cum esset
annorum XVI, amicitia coepit uti Annaei Cornuti, ita ut
nusquam ab eo discederet; inductus aliquatenus in philo-
15 sophiam est.
   amicos habuit a prima adulescentia Caesium Bassum
poetam et Calpurnium Staturam, qui vivo eo iuvenis
decessit. coluit ut patrem Servilium Nonianum. cognovit
per Cornutum etiam Annaeum Lucanum, aeque tum audi-
20 torem Cornuti. nam Cornutus illo tempore tragicus fuit
sectae poeticae, qui libros philosophiae reliquit. sed Luca-
nus mirabatur adeo scripta Flacci, ut vix se retineret
recitantem a clamore: quae illius essent vera esse poemata,
se ludos facere. sero cognovit et Senecam, sed non ut
25 caperetur eius ingenio. usus est apud Cornutum duorum
convictu doctissimorum et sanctissimorum virorum acriter
tunc philosophantium, Claudi Agathini medici Lacedae-

LIFE OF AULES PERSIUS FLACCUS, TAKEN FROM THE COMMENTARY OF VALERIUS PROBUS[1]

Aules Persius Flaccus was born December 4th, in the consulship of Fabius Persicus and L. Vitellius (34 A.D.) and died November 24th in the consulship of P. Marius and Afinius Gallus (62 A.D.).

Born at Volaterrae in Etruria, he was a Roman Knight,[2] related by blood and marriage to persons of the first rank. He died on his estates eight miles down the Via Appia.

His father died leaving him orphaned at the age of six. Fulvia Sisennia[3] later married the Roman knight Fusius, and buried him too within a few years.

Flaccus was educated at Volaterrae until he was twelve. Thereafter at Rome he received his secondary education from Remmius Palaemon and his training in rhetoric from Verginius Flavus. From the age of sixteen he entered the company of Annaeus Cornutus[4], being constantly with him and receiving a measure of instruction in philosophy.

From early adolescence he was friendly with Caesius Bassus the poet, and with Calpurnius Statura who died young in Persius' lifetime. He had a filial regard for Servilius Nonianus. Through Cornutus he was acquainted also with Annaeus Lucanus,[5] likewise a pupil of Cornutus's at the time. For in those days Cornutus was a tragedian of the poetic school and left books on philosophy.[6] But Lucan had such an admiration for Flaccus's work that, while reciting, he scarcely refrained from crying out that what came from his pen was true poetry whilst his own compositions were bagatelles. Late in life he came to know Seneca[7] also. However, he did not find his personality engaging. In company with Cornutus he met on familiar terms two learned and upright gentlemen of his day, devoted philosophers — Claudius Agathinus of Lacedaemon, the physician,

---

1. Whose identity is discussed by Ja pp.CXXXVIff.
2. On the meaning and implications of this title see OCD *equites,* P. Garnsey, *Social Status and Legal Privilege in the Roman Empire* (Oxford, 1970), pp.237-40.
3. The meaning is, for whatever reason, incompletely expressed. This is the name of P.'s mother, as the Anc. Comm. on Sat. 6.6 tells us.
4. Stoic philosopher, teacher and writer, see VE pp.47-102, cf. Sat. 5, init.
5. The poet Lucan.
6. So the MSS. Edd. have proposed various emendations of this sentence or the excision of all of it and of the first word of the next. In the following sentence 'that what came ... etc.' translates a version constructed out of a very confused set of MS readings and 'while reciting' has been doubted.
7. Seneca the Younger, philosopher, poet and tutor to Nero.

monii et Petroni Aristocratis Magnetis, quos unice miratus
est et aemulatus, cum aequales essent Cornuti, minor ipse.
30 idem decem fere annis summe dilectus a Paeto Thrasea est,
ita ut peregrinaretur quoque cum eo aliquando, cognatam
eius Arriam uxorem habente.

    fuit morum lenissimorum, verecundiae virginalis, famae
pulchrae, pietatis erga matrem et sororem et amitam ex-
35 emplo sufficientis. fuit frugi, pudicus.

    reliquit circa HS vicies matri et sorori. scriptis tantum
ad matrem codicillis Cornuto rogavit ut daret HS $\overline{XX}$, aut
ut quidam, $\bar{C}$; ut alii volunt, et argenti facti pondo viginti
et libros circa septingentos Chrysippi sive bibliothecam
40 suam omnem. verum Cornutus sublatis libris pecuniam
sororibus, quas heredes frater fecerat, reliquit.

    scriptitavit et raro et tarde; hunc ipsum librum inper-
fectum reliquit. versus aliqui dempti sunt ultimo libro, ut
quasi finitus esset. leviter contraxit Cornutus et Caesio
45 Basso, petenti ut ipse ederet, tradidit edendum. scripserat
in pueritia Flaccus etiam praetextam †vescio et opericon†
librum unum et paucos [sororum Thraseae] in Arriam
matrem versus, quae se ante virum occiderat. omnia ea
auctor fuit Cornutus matri eius ut aboleret. editum librum
50 continuo mirari homines et diripere coeperunt.

    decessit autem vitio stomachi anno aetatis XXX.

    sed mox ut a schola magistrisque devertit, lecto Lucili
libro decimo vehementer saturas componere instituit.
cuius libri principium imitatus est, sibi primo, mox omni-
55 bus detrectaturus cum tanta recentium poetarum et ora-
torum insectatione, ut etiam Neronem illius temporis
principem inculpaverit. cuius versus in Neronem cum ita
se haberet: *auriculas asini Mida rex habet*, in eum modum a
Cornuto, ipse tantummodo, est emendatus: *auriculas asini*
60 *quis non habet?* ne hoc in se Nero dictum arbitraretur.

and Petronius Aristocrates from Magnesia. He admired them especially, and found them an example, for they were of Cornutus's generation and he was younger. For a period of about ten years he was a special favourite with Paetus Thrasea[8] and even travelled abroad with him sometimes. Thrasea's wife, Arria,[8] was the poet's relative.

He had a most gentle character, a modesty that was virginal and an untarnished reputation. His care for his mother, sister and aunt would serve as an example. He was temperate and chaste.

He left about two million sesterces[9] to his mother and sister. In a codicil addressed only to his mother he requested her to present Cornutus with twenty thousand sesterces, or, according to some, with a hundred thousand.[10] According to others she was further to give him twenty pounds' weight of wrought silver and about seven hundred volumes of Chrysippus, his entire library. Cornutus, however, took the books and left the money to the sisters whom their brother had made his heirs.

He wrote both infrequently and slowly, and left even this book unfinished. A number of lines were removed from the end of the book to give it the appearance of completeness. Cornutus shortened it slightly and handed it over for publication to Caesius Bassus who requested that the task should be his in person. In his boyhood he had written an historical drama, *The †Vescio,*[11] a single book of *†Operica*[11] and some verses upon the elder Arria who had killed herself in front of her husband[12]. Cornutus advised Persius's mother that she should destroy all this material. When it appeared his book immediately met with admiration and a ready sale.

He died of a stomach complaint in his thirtieth[13] year.

Then, when he left school and his teachers, he read the tenth book of Lucilius and enthusiastically began to compose satires. He imitated the beginning of this book, proceeding to denigrate himself first,then everyone else, and satirising recent poets and orators to the extent that he found fault even with Nero, the reigning emperor. A verse of his against Nero read "King Midas has ass's ears". Cornutus emended that line (but no other) thus: "Who's not got ass's ears?" so that Nero should not think it was against him. [14]

---

8. Well-known representatives of Stoicism, see VE pp.33-43, OCD s.v. *Arria Minor,* cf. n.12.

9. 400,000 sesterces was the amount needed to qualify for the rank of Knight.

10. The MSS suggest the figures 2,000,000 and 10,000,000 which must be corrupt, see Cl p.xxvi. The authenticity and truth of the two following sentences has been suspected.

11. The titles are uncertain, see the textual apparatus in VP, Cl, and the nn. of Bo.

12. See Plin. *Ep.* 3.16. She was the mother of the Arria mentioned previously. The excised words (*sororum Thraseae* meaningless; *socrum Thraseae*, 'Thrasea's mother-in-law', Cas.) were perhaps originally a note to this effect.

13. 'Twenty-ninth' would be accurate, cf. Jerome in Cl's apparatus. The numeral could fairly easily have been mis-written, cf. VP.

14. The authenticity of this final paragraph lies under heavy suspicion, cf. VP pp.V, X, 10f. The line of the Satires referred to is 1.121 on which see Appx. A(i), p.97.

Appendix F
Bibliographical Information, Table of Manuscript-Symbols, List of Abbreviations

1. General

Bibliographical surveys of material on Persius (including bibliographies) are provided by both Bo (pp. XXVII-XXXVIII) and B (pp. 129-33). For recent decades there are bibliographies by V.. D'Agostino; RSC 6.1958.63-72 (for 1946-57) and RSC 11.1963.54-64 (for 1957-62); and, within surveys of material on satire in general, by W. S. Anderson, CW 50.1956.37f. (for 1937-55), CW 57.1964.344-6 (for 1955-62) and CW 63.1970.191-4, 199 (for 1962-68). These are now printed in *The Classical World Bibliography of Roman Drama and Poetry and Ancient Fiction*, New York, 1978. See too Knoche pp. 170f., 207f., 224-6. The yearly volumes *L'Année Philologique* (ed. J. Marouzeau, Paris, Les belles Lettres, 1928- still in progress) may also be consulted.

In preparing this translation I have used mainly the celebrated edition of Jahn (Leipzig, 1843: Ja) together with those of Conington-Nettleship (Oxford, 1893: CN) and Dolç (Barcelona, 1949: D) and have sought further help from other editions mentioned in footnotes and, where abbreviated, in the list of abbreviations. H. Beikircher *Kommentar zur VI. Satire des A Persius Flaccus* (Wien, 1969: B) and J. C. Bramble, *Persius and the Programmatic Satire* (Cambridge, 1974: Br) have been invaluable tutors on their two satires and in other things.

The wording of my Latin text is closely based upon that of W. V. Clausen (*A. Persi Flacci Saturarum Liber,* Oxford, 1956: Cl). My textual apparatus derives from his and uses his manuscript-symbols (cf. below). Its usual aim is simply to list any variant from among the readings assembled by C1 which I have not chosen and which, if adopted, would make sense. This serves to indicate throughout, most importantly at points where there are difficulties of interpretation, the possibilities that are immediately available. In the absence of variants of other kinds the symbol Φ, which I have often allowed to stand, signifies *a* majority of the seven manuscripts CGLMNRW and there is no means of knowing the size of the majority or what members of the group constitute it; and in general my apparatus is not a reliable base for detailed discussion of the text, which must be based on the Introduction and Apparatuses of Clausen's two editions — the one mentioned above and the Oxford Classical Text of 1959.

Professor N. Rudd's lucid translation (*The Satires of Horace and Persius,* Harmondsworth, 1973), with its excellent introduction and notes, is a work that readily gives the clearest possible account of P.'s meaning.

2. Table of Manuscript-Symbols used in the Textual Apparatus

P	*Montepessulanus 125, Pithoeanus*	b	*Bernensis 398*
A	*Montepessulanus 212*	c	*Bernensis 542*
B	*Vaticanus tabularii basilicae H 36*	d	*Bernensis 648*
a	Consensus of A and B	e	*Parisinus 8048*
Bob.	Palimpsest fragment, provenance	f	*Laurentianus 68. 24*
	Bobbio, *fragmentum Vaticanum 5750*	h	*Parisinus 8272*
Sang.	*Sangallensis 870* (a florilegium)	k	*Parisinus 8049*
V	*Vaticanus Reginensis 1560*	n	*Norimbergensis*
C	*Parisinus 8055*	p	*Parisinus 8070*
G	*Bernensis 257*	q	*Leidensis Vossianus 13*
L	*Leidensis bibl. publ. 78*	r	*Vaticanus Reginensis 1562*
M	*Monacensis 23577*	s	*Vindobonensis 85*
N	*Monacensis 14498*	u	*Vindobonensis 131*
R	*Laurentianus 37. 19*	x	*Vaticanus Palatinus 1710*
W	*Monacensis 330*		
Φ	Consensus of a majority of CGLMNRW		

Citations of the text from the Ancient Commentary (Σ) which appears in the MSS L and M and also in U (*Monacensis 14482*) are given thus: Σ(L), Σ(MU) etc. Σ on its own indicates the consensus of Σ(L M and U).

The Introduction to W. V. Clausen, *A. Persi Flacci Saturarum Liber,* Oxford, 1956, gives the dates of these manuscripts and discusses their nature and their relative values as evidence for the text. Manuscripts cited only occasionally are named in a less abbreviated form and are usually to be found listed in the same work, p. 40f. Further information in Ja pp. CLXXIII-CCXVI, although see Cl p.xvi. On names, origins and locations of manuscripts F. W. Hall, *A Companion to Classical Texts* (Oxford, 1913) ch. IX is helpful.

3. Select List of Abbreviations

Abbreviations of ancient authors' names and works are listed only where they cannot reasonably be guessed with such help as necessary from lists of abbreviations or of authors in, for example, *The Oxford Latin Dictionary.*
Editions of Latin authors may generally be traced in the Supplementary Bibliographies appended by A. M. Duff to J. W. Duff, *A Literary History of Rome* (2 vols.), London, 1960 and 1964; or in OCD².
Publication-details of periodicals are usually those listed as current in *L'Année Philologique* (see p.124) 46.1975, pp. XIII ss.; those of earlier issues may sometimes be different.)

Abergl.   O. Jahn, *Über den Aberglauben des bösen Blicks bei den Alten,* Berichte über die Verhandl. der Königl. sächs. Ges. der Wissensch. zu Leipz., Bd. 7 (Leipzig 1855) pp. 28ff.

(Ps.-)Acr.   Ancient commentary on Horace, going under the name of Helenius Acro see OCD.

a. (h.) l.   ad (hunc) locum, on the (this) passage. Gives a reference to the passage just mentioned in a note.

AJP   *American Journal of Philology,* Baltimore, Johns Hopkins Press.

Anc. Comm.   Ancient Commentary; notes (scholia) on the Satires, copied in some MSS, see p. 125, Cl pp.xiv, xxiiis. There is (see C1) no reliable edition of the Anc. Comm. I have occasionally taken notes which seemed especially apposite from the versions offered by Ja, Buecheler.

Anth. Lat. Anthologia Latina . . . ediderunt F. Buecheler et A. Riese, 5 fasc., Leipzig 1894-1926.

ap.   *apud,* in, giving reference to an author's work.

A.P.   The Greek Anthology (*Anthologia Palatina*), see OCD² s.v. *Anthology.*

App. Crit.   The Critical Apparatus of manuscript-readings beneath the Latin Text.

B   H. Beikircher, *Kommentar zur VI. Satire des A. Persius Flaccus,* Wien, 1969.

Baehrens PLM   *Poetae Latini Minores* vols. I-V ed. E. Baehrens, Leipzig, 1879-83.

Balsdon   J.P.V.D. Balsdon, *Life and Leisure in Anc. Rome,* London, 1969.

Becker, Becker('s) *Gallus*   W. A. Becker (trans. P. Metcalfe) *Gallus,* London, 1849

Bennett   C. E. Bennett, *Syntax of Early Latin* (2 vols.), Boston, 1910, 1914.

Blümner   H. Blümner, *Die Römischen Privataltertümer*, München, 1911.

Bo   D. Bo (ed.) *A. Persi Flacci Saturarum Liber*, Paravia, 1969.

Bonner, *Declamation*   S. F. Bonner, *Roman Declamation in the Late Republic and Early Empire*, Liverpool, 1949.

Bonner, *Education*   S. F. Bonner, *Education in Ancient Rome*, London, 1977.

Br   J. C. Bramble, *Persius and the Programmatic Satire*, Cambridge, 1974.

BRLS   W. W. Buckland, *The Roman Law of Slavery*, Cambridge, 1908.

Buckland TBORL[3]   W. W. Buckland, *A Textbook of Roman Law*, 3rd Ed. by P. Stein, Cambridge, 1963.

Buecheler   *A. Persi Flacci, D. Iunii Iuvenalis... Saturae* rec. O. Jahn, ed. altera F. Buecheler, Berlin, 1886.

Cas.   I. Casaubon (ed.), *Auli Persii Flacci Satirarum Liber*, Paris, 1605: an enlarged edition by his son, M. Casaubon (Leyden, 1695) is accessible in the edn. of Duebner (see below) from which references are taken.

C.C.A.G.   *Catalogus Codicum Astrologorum Graecorum*, 12 vols., Brussels,1898-1953 (see Manilius, *Astronomica* ed. G. P. Goold, LCL, 1978, p. cxvi).

CIL   *Corpus Inscriptionum Latinarum*, consilio... Acad. Lit. Regiae Borussicae editum, 16 vols., Suppll., Berlin, 1863 -.

CJ   *The Classical Journal*, Athens, Univ. of Georgia.

Cl   W. V. Clausen (ed.), *A. Persi Flacci Saturarum Liber, Accedit Vita*, Oxford, 1956.

CN   *The Satires of A. Persius Flaccus*, Trans. and Comm. by J. Conington, ed. H. Nettleship, Oxford, 1893. (Hildesheim 1967).

Coffey   M. Coffey, *Roman Satire*, London, 1976.

CP   *Classical Philology*, Chicago, Univ. of Chicago Press.

CQ   *Classical Quarterly*, Oxford, Oxford Univ. Press.

CR   *Classical Review*, Oxford, Oxford Univ. Press.

ctr.   'contrast'.

CW   *The Classical World* (up to 1956, *The Classical Weekly*), Bethlehem, Pa., Lehigh Univ.

D   M. Dolç (ed.), *A. Persio Flacco, Sátiras*, Barcelona, 1949.

Dessen   Cynthia S. Dessen, *Iunctura Callidus Acri: A Study of Persius' Satires*, Illinois Studd. in Lang. and Lit. 59, Urbana, 1968.

De Vogel   C. J. De Vogel, *Greek Philosophy, A Collection of Texts* (Vols. I[3], II[3], III[2]), Leiden, 1963-7.

Dict. d'Archéol. Chrét.   F. Cabrol and H. Leclercq, edd., *Dictionnaire d'Archéolgie Chrétienne et de Liturgie*, Paris, 1924-53.

DS   Ch. Daremberg and Edm. Saglio, *Dictionnaire des Antiquités Grecques et Romaines* (5 vols.), Paris, 1873-1919.

Duebner   *Auli Persii Flacci Satirarum Liber cum . . . Isaaci Casauboni Notis . . . Auxit F. Duebner,* Leipzig, 1833, repr. Osnabrück, 1972.

Encycl. Brit.   *Encyclopaedia Britannica* (15th Ed.), Chicago, London, 1974.

Forcellini, *Lex.*   A. Forcellini, *Totius Latinitatis Lexicon* (Engl. Edn., *Tot. Lat. Lex. Jacobi Facciolati . . .A. Forcellini* ed. J. Bailey, London, 1828).

Friedländer, RLM   L. Friedländer (trans. L. A. Magnus and others), *Roman Life and Manners under the Early Empire,* 4 vols., London [1908]-1913.

GLK   *Grammatici Latini,* ed. H. Keil, 7 vols., Suppl., Leipzig, 1855-80.

Gnomon   *Gnomon : Kritische Zeitschrift für Altertumswissenschaft,* München, Beck.

GR   *Greece and Rome,* Oxford, Clarendon Press.

Hermes   *Hermes: Zeitschrift für klassische Philologie,* Wiesbaden, Steiner.

Housman, *Classical Papers*   *The Classical Papers of A. E. Housman,* ed. J. Diggle, F.R.D. Goodyear, 3 vols., Cambridge, 1972.

ILS   *Inscriptiones Latinae Selectae,* ed. H. Dessau, 3 vols., Berlin, 1892-1916.

Ioh. Saresb.   Iohannes Saresberiensis, John of Salisbury (Migne, *Patrol. Lat.* vol. 199.1ff.).

Ja   O. Jahn (ed.), *Auli Persii Flacci Satirarum Liber,* Leipzig, 1843, Hildesheim, 196[

Jahn 1886 See Buecheler.

J. Philol.   Journal of Philology, London and Cambridge.

JRS   *Journal of Roman Studies,* London, 31-34 Gordon Square.

Kamb., Kambylis   A. Kambylis, *Die Dichterweihe u. ihre Symbolik,* Heidelberg, 1965.

KH   *Q. Horatius Flaccus, Oden u. Epoden*[8]*, Satire*[6]*, Briefe*[5], 3 vols., ed. A. Kiessling, R. Heinze . . . Nachwort von E. Burck, Berlin, 1955-7.

Knoche   U. Knoche, *Roman Satire (Die römische Satire,* 3rd German edition, Gottingen, 1971) tr. S. Ramage, Bloomington, 1975.

Korzeniewski   D. Korzeniewski, *Die erste Satire des P.* in *Die römische Satire* (ed. by him), Darmstadt, 1970.

Kroll, *Stud.* W. Kroll, *Studien zum Verständnis der römischen Literatur,* Stuttgart, 1924.

Kugler   W. Kugler, *Des Persius Wille zu sprachlicher Gestaltung in seiner Wirkung auf Ausdruck und Komposition,* Würzburg, 1940.

Latomus   *Latomus: Revue d'études latines,* Bruxelles, 60, rue Colonel-Chaltin.

LCL   Loeb Classical Library.

Lejay   P. Lejay (ed.), *Oeuvres d'Horace: Satires,* Paris, 1911.

LHS   (M. Leumann), J.B. Hoffman, A. Szantyr, *Lateinische Syntax u Stilistik,* München, 1965. (Handbuch der Altertumswissenschaft, 2 Abt., 2 Teil, 2 Band.)

LS   C. T. Lewis and C. Short, *A Latin Dictionary,* Oxford, 1879.

L-S   H. G. Liddell and R. Scott, *A Greek-English Lexicon,* new ed. H. S. Jones, R. Mackenzie, Oxford, 1925-40.

M (e.g. fr. 2M)   Morel, see below.

Mayor (Juv.)   *Thirteen Satires of Juvenal,* ed. J. E. B. Mayor, 2 vols., London, 1872, 1878.

Migne (*Patrol. Graec.*)   J. P. Migne, ed. *Patrologiae cursus completus . . . series graeca* (161 vols.), Paris, 1857-1903.

Migne (*Patrol. Lat.*)   J. P. Migne, ed. *Patrologiae cursus completus . . . series latina* (221 vols.), Paris, 1845-1904 (also Suppll.)

MM   J. Marquardt, *Das Privatleben der Römer,* 2nd ed. by A. Mau, 2 vols., Leipzig, 1886.

Mnemos.   Mnemosyne, Leiden, Brill.

Morel FPL   W. Morel (ed.), *Fragmenta Poetarum Latinorum,* Leipzig, 1927.

Müller, DRM   L. Mueller, *De Re Metrica Poetarum Latinorum praeter Plautum et Terentium Libri Septem,* Leipzig 1894 (Hildesheim, 1967)

Mus. Helv.   Museum Helveticum, Basel, Schwabe.

Nem.   G. Némethy (ed.), *A. Persii Flacci Satirae,* Budapest, 1903.

Nisbet   R.G.M. Nisbet, *Persius,* in J. P. Sullivan (ed.), *Critical Essays on Roman Literature: Satire,* London, 1963.

OCD, OCD[2]   *The Oxford Classical Dictionary,* Oxford, 1949, (2nd ed. 1970).

OLD   *Oxford Latin Dictionary,* Oxford, 1968-

Otto, *Sprichw.* A. Otto, *Die Sprichwörter u. sprichwörtlichen Redensarten der Römer,* Leipzig, 1890.

P.   Persius.

PCPhS   Procc. of the Cambridge Philological Society, Cambridge Univ. Press.

Philol.   *Philologus,* Zeitschr. für klassische Philologie, Berlin, Akademie-Verlag.

Ph.Q.   *Philological Quarterly,* Iowa Univ. Press.

Platner-Ashby   S. B. Platner, T. Ashby, *A Topographical Dictionary of Anc. Rome,* London, 1929.

PNH   C. Plinius Secundus (Pliny the Elder), *Naturalis Historia.*

Pohlenz   M. Pohlenz, *Die Stoa: Geschichte einer geistigen Bewegung* (2 vols.), Göttingen, 1948-9, 3rd edn., 1964.

Porph.   Porphyrion, 3rd Cent. A.D., Commentator on Horace, see OCD.

Pretor   A. Pretor (ed.), *A Persii Flacci Satirarum Liber,* Cambridge, 1907.

PW   A. F. Pauly, G. Wissowa (and others, edd.), *Realencyclopädie der classischen Altertumswissenschaft* (49 vols.), Stuttgart 1893-1972 (also Suppll.).

Ramsay   *Juvenal and Persius . . . English Translation* by G. G. Ramsay, (LCL), Revised ed. 1940.

Ramus   Ramus, *Critical Studies in Greek and Latin Literature,* Clayton, Victoria (Aus.), Monash Univ.

REL   *Revue des Etudes Latines,* Paris, Les Belles Lettres.

Rh.M.   *Rheinisches Museum,* Frankfurt, Sauerländer.

RIGI   *Rivista Indo-Greca-Italica di filologia, lingua, antichità,* Naples.

RIL   *Rendiconti dell' Istituto Lombardo, Classe di Lettere, Scienze morali e storiche,* Milan.

ROL   *Remains of Old Latin,* ed. and trans. by E. H. Warmington (LCL, 4 vols.), London, 1935-40.

RSC   *Rivista di Studi Classici,* Turin, 16 Via S. Pio v.

Rudd   N. Rudd (tr.), *The Satires of Horace and Persius* (Penguin Classics), Harmondsworth, 1973.

Σ   Scholia, see next item, also Table of Manuscript-Symbols, p.125.

Schol.   Scholium, Scholia, see Anc. Comm.

Schol. Juv.   *Scholia in Iuvenalem vetustiora,* ed. P. Wessner, Leipzig, 1931.

Sciv.   N. Scivoletto (ed.), *Auli Persi Flacci Saturae*[2], Florence, 1961.

S-H   M. Schanz (extensively revised by C. Hosius, G. Krüger) *Geschichte der römischen Literatur* (4 vols.), München, 1914-35.

sts.   Sometimes.

Summers   W. C. Summers, ed., *Select Letters of Seneca,* London, 1932.

SVF   *Stoicorum Veterum Fragmenta* coll. J. von Arnim, Leipzig, 1921-4.

TLL   *Thesaurus Linguae Latinae* (Vols. I-IX.2.5., in progress) Leipzig, 1900-

V (V.*E,* V.*G,* V.*A*)   Vergil (*Eclogues, Georgics, Aeneid*).

V³   E. Vahlen, *Ennianae Poesis Reliquiae* (3rd Ed.), Leipzig, 1928.

VE   F. Villeneuve, *Essai sur Perse,* Paris, 1918.

VP   *A. Persii Flacci satirae . . . texte . . . commentaire . . .* par
      F. Villeneuve, Paris, 1918.

Warmington, *Nero*   B. H. Warmington, *Nero, Reality and Legend,* London, 1969.

Wilson AR   L. M. Wilson, *The Clothing of the Anc. Romans,* Baltimore, 1938.

WZUR   *Wissenschaftliche Zeitschrift der Universität Rostock* (Jahrgang 15, 1966,
      Heft 4/5 contains the Papers read at an international conference on the theme
      "Römische Satire u. römische Gesellschaft", held in May, 1965. Summaries in
      German, Russian, English and French are added.)

YCS   *Yale Classical Studies,* New Haven, Yale Univ. Press.

ARIS & ℞ PHILLIPS LTD

ASSICAL STUDIES *(Cloth)*

.E. Fisher
BRIS: A study in the values of Honour
Shame in Ancient Greece

V. Johnston
ADEMARKS ON GREEK VASES

. Lazenby
NNIBAL'S WAR: A military history

Markotic (ed.)
CIENT EUROPE AND THE MEDITERR-
EAN: Studies in honour of Hugh Hencken

. Mee
ODES IN THE BRONZE AGE

Proctor
E EXPERIENCE OF THUCYDIDES

. Sanders
MAN CRETE: An Archaeological Survey
Gazateer of the period 69BC to 824AD

. Trypanis (translated by W.W. Phelps)
E HOMERIC EPICS

Walcot
VY AND THE GREEKS

ginia Webb
CHAIC GREEK FAIENCE: Miniature
ects from East Greece 650-500 BC

.A. Wilson
ILY UNDER THE ROMAN EMPIRE

CLASSICAL TEXTS *(cloth and limp bound)*

Joan Booth
OVID - AMORES II: A literary commentary
with Text and Translation

J.R. Jenkinson
PERSIUS - THE SATIRES: Text and anno-
tated Translation

R. Mayer
LUCAN - CIVIL WAR VIII: a literary com-
mentary with Text and Translation

Plato (ed. R.G. Bury)
THE SYMPOSIUM: Text with critical notes
and commentary

A.H. Sommerstein
THE COMEDIES OF ARISTOPHANES
A New Series of Editions
VOL. 1: ARCHARNIANS
VOL. 2: KNIGHTS

J. Wilson
PYLOS 425 BC: Thucydides' text with a his-
torical and topographical study of the campaign

*Details and catalogues available from the Publishers, Aris & Phillips
Ltd., Teddington House, Church Street, Warminster, Wilts, England.*